HENRY HOOK'S
CRYPTIC
CROSSWORDS

VOLUME
1

TIMES

BOOKS

ISBN 0-8129-2767-2

Random House Website address:
http://www.randomhouse.com/

Text design by Mark Frnka
Manufactured in the United States of America
2 4 6 8 9 7 5 3
First Edition

INTRODUCTION

Oh, it's you.

Welcome to *Henry Hook's Cryptic Crosswords Volume 1*, the first in a new series of cryptic-crossword books from Times Books. (Actually, it's the third, but all the puzzles in those first two were reprints, so they don't count.)

If you're familiar with my previous ventures in the world of crypticdom, then the assortment of bafflers herein should present little or no difficulty for you. If you're not, where the heck ya been?

At any rate, you can expect the usual array of wordplay (anagrams, homonyms, charades, etc.), plus a few tricks I'd never thought of before — there's even one puzzle that's completely written in the Cyrillic alphabet. No, that's not true. Maybe in the next book.

Excuse me, there's my doorbell.

Sorry. Now then, where was I? Oh, yes, I've also included a generous variety of gimmickry in the diagrams as well as in the clues. Some answers have to be entered with letters omitted, or converted into numbers, or in crayon, or some such silliness. (P.S. — I lied about the crayon.) In fact, there's even one puzzle in which all the answers are — well, never mind; you'll recognize it when you get there.

By the way, in the spirit of orneriness, I've neglected to tell you when a puzzle's answers include proper names, British spellings, foreign words, archaisms, and the like. You're smart people — you don't need my help.

I would like to express my thanks and acknowledgments to such folks as Emily Cox and Henry Rathvon, E. R. Galli and Richard Maltby, Jr., Stephen Sondheim, Mike Shenk, Fraser Simpson, the various puzzlewriters for Britain's *The Listener* and *The Observer,* and anyone else whose ideas I've blatantly pilfered.

I hope you enjoy solving *Henry Hook's Cryptic Crosswords Volume 1*, because if you don't, there won't be a next volume, and Times Books will cancel my contract, and I'll lose a ton of money, and my landlord will kick me out, and I'll wind up out on the street begging for spare change, and it'll be YOUR FAULT!!!

Happy solving!

Henry Hook

1
START OF SOMETHING BIG

Except for its size, this is a standard cryptic crossword.

ACROSS

1 In France, novel masks belonging to Thatcher, perhaps (7)
5 Freshly invigorated, Coty took a mate (7)
9 Checking New Testament, rewrite the last Commandment (5)
12 Money alien's removed from pails (5)
13 Sorry about destruction at rear of building (5)
14 Around mid-January, hunting tailless marine creature (3,6)
15 Stick around — almost cure man with liqueur (5,2,6)
16 In Chicago, nine overweight people taking ''Intro to Home Economics'' (3,4)
17 Those who authorize documents with new seals (8)
18 Narrowmindedness shown by head of Teamsters' Union, inhibiting unknown rock singer (6,6)
21 Piece of beef picked up and cooked (7)
23 Each expert has a type of chart (6)
25 Hot dogs finally given to Leonard (6)
28 Type paragraph on chief of staff's benevolence (10)
30 Renegade gets to America, adopting cause (10)
32 Church backs election in trade school (2-4)
33 Follow mid-Westerner out of big house (6)
34 Sickening-sweetness in remake of *Electra* (7)
37 Interrupting the workday to get drunk — that's astonishing (12)
39 *MASH* actor in a slicker (8)
42 In fixed procedure, prepared floral arrangement (7)
44 Yours truly, playing first piece from Strauss, following one hundred string musicians (13)
46 With great effort, two people (you and me) will get in early, devoid of energy (9)
47 Walk in rain cut short by religious leader (5)
48 Border guards scratch here and there (5)
49 King spotted returning to low-down joints? (5)
50 Japanese guitar is in no different condition, ultimately (7)
51 Dotty has to insult some campers (7)

DOWN

1 Old fiddle is placed in here, because . . . (5)
2 . . . band makes stranger roar about box (9)
3 Gob to regret picking up rubber? (7)
4 Going on and on about closing of sewer grating (5-7)
5 Assailant runs around assistant (6)
6 Such timing is off in nocturne (5,5)
7 My group, back in horse opera (7)
8 Awfully isolated heartthrob, in part? (8)
9 Stipend, with a raise, accepted by frugal band with nearly new number (5-5-3)
10 Noted pacifist . . . in retrospect, the original chicken? (5)
11 Actively participating in H.'s family business? (5-2)
17 Author of a half-hearted book written in November (7)
19 Northern dwelling ''C'' occupied by grand lady (5)
20 Head of navy, cruising around Honolulu, ultimately gets *mal de mer* (6)
22 Requests awards following one's performances (13)
24 Perhaps trim ends of hair in advance (6)
26 Cragman's final climb, in the early stages (7)
27 Old Tunisian wagon hand almost guards against one (12)
29 After all, it sounds like a long study session in British compound (5)
31 Thick-skinned one has the potential to be rich sooner (10)
35 $100 springs doubled in disreputable garages (4,5)
36 Nonbelievers at robberies (8)
37 Book written about citified city (7)
38 Poet has center of baked potato stuffed with grass (7)
40 Due to splash in a pond (7)
41 In African land, leader of resistance to take hold (4,2)
43 Son to do nothing but move laterally (5)
45 Dress suits in position (5)

2

CROSSWORDS

Unclued answers follow an obvious pattern.

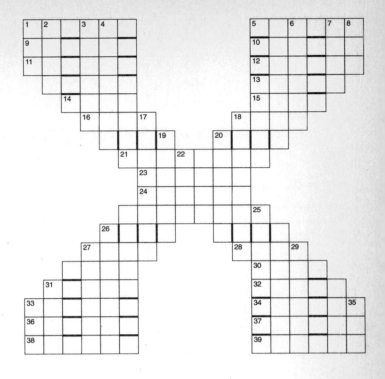

ACROSS

1 Holy man, 100% reflective, breaks out (6)
5 Garment on a large virgin (6)
9 In front of beer nuts (6)
10 *Roots* author offers to let off steam? (6)
11 Tavern uprising, for the most part, in Latin Quarter? (6)
12 Poet, swallowing iron, got sick (6)
13 Get together for a church service (5)
14 Without a bit of capriciousness, choose a rabbitlike animal (4)
15 Business letters from terminal in E-mail (4)
16 Singer improvised a lot (4)
18 Couple left in kitchen (4)
21 Titan is overexcited, just a bit (8)
23 Stoneworkers working in large quantity (6)
24 Rhetorically florid talk about frontal nudity (6)
27 Endlessly pretty European city (4)
28 Portion of the brain, half the time (4)
30 Be contrary during golden years (4)
31 Shelters nearly a dozen on back street (5)
32 Derelict wakes in a contorted position (5)
33 Debut of *Moulin Rouge* reviewed in reference file (6)
34 I nearly uttered a word of delight for prophet (6)
36 They have uncapped depressants (6)
37 Four out of five wield the scepter as a punishment device (6)
38 Responsibilities of people outside America (6)
39 Ill-tempered Conservative governed Kentucky (6)

DOWN

1 Fall evening beginning with a short walk? (3)
2 Harvest is essential to agriculture, apparently (4)
3 Female attorney left Iowa (6)
4 John left by eastern stream (7)
6 Radius in limb became smaller (6)
7 Drinks and feels awful, reportedly (4)
8 Guided missile discharged from within (3)
13 Strange man discovered suppressing story (5)
17 It's a contradiction, oddly — no room to accommodate two unknown characters (8)
18 John somehow needs to be relaxed (8)
19 Let off steam, at first — father gets madder (6)
20 Young detective can box (6)
22 Slave seen misbehaving (4)
25 Cheese served up by a pair: $1,000 (5)
26 Means of causing great pain or utter chaos (7)
27 Begins swinging bats (6)
29 In bank, a racketeer's capital (6)
33 $1,000.00 is low (3)
35 Greeting the man at end of day (3)

3
GOING DOWN

One Down answer in each column is to be entered with one of its letters dropped to the square at the bottom of the column. These letters will then reveal why they have dropped.

ACROSS

1 Gift wrapping work is difficult (7)
7 *Times* features wonderful photographer (5)
11 Stick is red, in part (6)
13 Discovered to be sort of green (5)
15 Everyone comes around to a coral reef (5)
16 "Fungus in a Can" a family member returned (7)
17 Giving medicine to soprano in performance (6)
18 The time being about a half-hour, it's out of the question (5)
20 Inclination to go topless and cast a spell (7)
22 Dismisses candidate's initial answer (4)
23 Southern singer's somersault (5)
25 Start of school . . . many openings (5)
28 After onset of snowstorm, guided toboggan (4)
30 Preferred to dress like a poor farmer (7)
32 Seeing red and gray buckles worn by Pole (5)
34 Taylor enters contest in foreign country (6)
36 Rod in an elaborately fashioned fireplace device (7)
37 Otherwise sad to tell about ego (5)
38 Semicircle(?) thus flipped by Shakespearean character (5)
39 Pair of troopers sheltered in Irish city (6)
40 Around end of competition, team becomes nasty (5)
41 President apprehended on Fourth of July (7)

DOWN

2 Engaged by sleuth's companion, yours truly serves (2 wds.)
3 Pension plan is crucial to leader of organization, we're told
4 *Globe* gives news about British pound
5 Surreptitiously agrees to accept senator's earliest bribes
6 Monk wearing oxygen mask
7 Outside of raccoon's tail, it's mostly black and white
8 Circle's radius, in general
9 Ted turned up carrying #10 machine part
10 In rye, a stimulant!
11 Amid quantities of brew, the Spanish will offer laments
12 After 2 o' clock, admits fools
14 Composer I saw penning Virginia reel's coda
19 Lid removed from vessels for grain
21 With a vengeance, consuming port
22 They're yellow, orange, and white, found in a pack
23 South American leper is a marathon runner
24 Absolutely true — going all around yard in return journey
26 Pressure bishop to leave Mideastern nation (2 wds.)
27 Open convertible? No luck
28 Frugal person has best interests at heart
29 Put together a system of belief about the essence of Uniatism
30 Begs for commendation from the audience
31 Sprite cavorting, I fear, with energy
33 Deception could become uglier if Republican is involved
34 Basketball star dribbled halfway up
35 Another word for "vivacity" in Japanese language

4

CROSSROADS

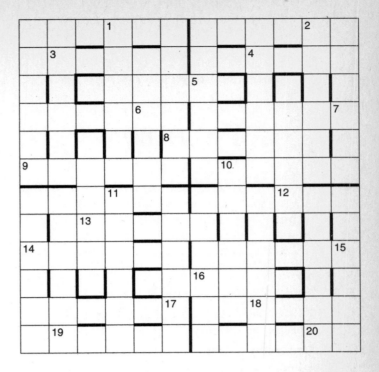

Each answer is six letters long. Clues are given in pairs; the answers in each pair intersect at the appropriate numbered square. Either the Across or the Down clue may appear first in any pair.

CLUES

1 Informed, by the way, about band of big animals
Dessert scrap rejected by Italian man

2 Muscle builder initially returned most of money
Chief of police makes more effective calls

3 Fiend did dances in performance
Think I'd had dinner? Not entirely

4 Mystery writer caught you concealing gun
Political group in New Jersey city after the first quarter

5 Unattractive woman back in love in brothel
British king and leader of expedition in canyon

6 Stiff fragment of redwood found in thicket
Slogan for gent backing paintings

7 Harmful condition of pennilessness?
Cooks left out of tributes

8 Ardor keeps half of guys in shape
Attack with faster explosive

9 Woman describes a 2,000-pounder?
Got out of bed, having got semi-deep sleep

10 Corrupt bosses haunt one's mind
Captain's observed retreating from inside war zone

11 Firmly implanted cross on the outskirts of the hollow
He makes music with small kitchen gadget

12 Deprived female wearing cap
$100 bid to get box for valuables

13 Steal a hot water pipe
Winds make sailing ships capsize

14 Tea balls drawn out
Driver sounded horn

15 Work with modern surveyor's assistants
Reportedly, you dubbed one

16 Former P.M. abolishes evil in meetinghouse
Male Dubliners like swampland

17 Back from the Orient, losing face
Violent kid consumes gin

18 About time — let out the herd?
Spunky eccentric comes around first

19 State champs make a selection
Stranger recalled German blitz (2 wds.)

20 Swimmer reeled wildly
Boisterous female gives call to sailors needing a refuge

5 ACROSTIC

CLUES

A Article found in sperm that's boiled (7) (21 101 78 116 29 187 90)

B Expensive to maintain Veteran's Administration in secrecy (7) (85 56 13 6 149 142 165)

C Civil War hero's all-purpose subsidy (12, 2 wds.) (175 136 34 59 159 107 125 12 66 199 190 153)

D Every preacher takes it to heart (4) (105 32 113 135)

E Cook in regular oven (5) (174 139 87 151 177)

F Ultimately, James Bond will hug little doll (7) (145 157 207 61 166 98 67)

G Cry out in disapproval, heated up about nothing (4) (58 185 180 73)

H Composer taken by couple back beyond B Street (9) (49 97 111 25 147 172 52 205 183)

I Holiday initially spent in diner (6) (171 15 123 28 118 144)

J I almost see restricting one's foolish acts (8) (7 33 48 204 148 119 86 62)

K Spanish gentleman, turning at sound of bell, taking a bow? (7) (112 133 27 91 11 200 40)

L Interrupted by strange echo, I work in cold storage place? (8) (46 65 188 2 176 129 161 160)

M To grunt . . . that is a challenge (7) (134 110 150 196 74 189 35)

N It's involved in scam . . . double-cross thwarts victim in an auspicious position (13, 2 wds.) (93 209 1 60 122 14 44 84 163 143 24 184 106)

O I used to broadcast in a remote place (7) (162 141 57 128 23 201 80)

P No aborigine eats half of eggs (8) (71 155 192 83 103 208 76 41)

Q Song about small back room (6) (17 26 55 79 94 156)

R Athletic club rowing team getting back last evening (11) (18 152 82 51 193 130 99 70 206 117 54)

S Star that's fallen in love with Dole before ceremony (9) (31 168 100 3 38 195 47 22 126)

T Go back into tent for a dairy product (6) (169 42 72 50 164 63)

U Poet's son hanged after rioting (9, 2 wds.) (9 191 115 89 69 182 127 36 104)

V Present . . . even after 40% price cut (7) (137 81 194 39 53 173 10)

W One mistake left story impossible to correct (11) (77 120 43 131 96 20 138 178 146 16 197)

X Family member found in New England — what a relief! (6) (108 158 124 154 203 19)

Y One man favored my group's driving force (7) (198 4 95 45 132 181 64)

Z Buried in rock, daughter has sore appearance, with regularity (11) (5 179 102 75 88 114 140 170 30 37 186)

AA Heeding jockeys, made a noise like a horse (7) (109 68 92 202 167 8 121)

1N	2L	3S		4Y	5Z	6B	7J	8AA		9U	10V	11K	12C	13B	14N	15I	16W	17Q	18R		19X	20W
21A		22S	23O	24N	25H	26Q	27K		28I	29A	30Z		31S	32D	33J	34C	35M	36U	37Z		38S	39V
	40K	41P	42T	43W	44N	45Y		46L	47S	48J		49H	50T	51R		52H	53V	54R	55Q	56B		57O
58G	59C		60N	61F	62J	63T		64Y	65L	66C	67F	68AA	69U	70R	71P	72T		73G	74M	75Z		76P
77W	78A	79Q	80O	81V	82R		83P	84N	85B	86J	87E	88Z	89U	90A		91K	92AA	93N	94Q	95Y	96W	97H
98F	99R	100S	101A	102Z		103P	104U	105D	106N		107C	108X	109AA	110M	111H	112K	113D	114Z	115U		116A	117R
118I	119J	120W		121AA	122N	123I	124X	125C	126S	127U	128O	129L	130R	131W		132Y	133K		134M	135D	136C	
137V	138W	139E	140Z	141O	142B	143N	144I	145F		146W	147H	148J	149B	150M	151E	152R		153C	154X	155P	156Q	
157F	158X	159C	160L		161L	162O	163N	164T	165B		166F	167AA	168S	169T		170Z	171I	172H	173V	174E		175C
176L	177E		178W	179Z	180G	181Y	182U	183H		184N	185G		186Z	187A	188L	189M	190C	191U		192P	193R	194V
195S	196M	197W		198Y	199C	200K	201O		202AA	203X	204J	205H	206R	207F		208P	209N					

6

HALF AND HALF

Each answer is to be divided exactly in half, with the first half going into the grid on the left and the second half into the grid on the right.

ACROSS
1 Marksman's drink (4)
4 Presented a sort of shirt and a sort of spat (6)
6 In a European country, you'll see carpenter closing wrench (6)
9 District worker in study (6)
10 Wild back-and-forth motion . . . turning sick inside (10)
11 Tender husband has drab clothing (6)
12 Relationship seen in outlines of sociology, zoology, and geology (6)
13 I must leave home up north — my, it's dark (6)
14 Lots of items on sale . . . a neat mix with 20% off estimate (10)
17 Small portion initially seemed sufficient (6)
20 Makes a big deal out of blunder during a CEO's TV broadcast (10)
21 Paper for *Time* edition (6)
22 Recently split . . . even heading for estrangement (6, 2 wds.)

25 Magicians were concealing explanation (6)
28 Northeastern airport described by *Observer*'s motto writers (10)
29 Dilapidated car — key's broken (6)
30 They're boring prophets, we're told (6)
31 Accepting conservative measure is not harmful (6)
32 Somewhat wholesome Spanish-language version of *Cheers*? (4)

DOWN
1 Scoring 100-0, playfully toss darts (6)
2 Roving sailor takes time to board British ship in bad weather (10)
3 Faxing without a cover letter, in conclusion (6)
4 Asks questions quietly about this new clerical position (10)
5 Area kept up outside Oregon's largest city (6)
7 Working with plaintiff's initial perjury (6)
8 Piece of jewelry is red, plated with green (4)
12 A boy ultimately enters repulsive places to disregard curfew (6, 2 wds.)
13 Rut or hole in orchard (6)
14 Carlos makes a slight alteration in seasonal music (6)
15 Story about a donkey and a dog (6)
16 ''The difference between males and females'' bugs a woman (6)
18 Act of threatening guys with a stick (10)
19 I'm upset by question in Kerouac novel — it's a bit of a shock (10)
23 String instrument owned by French musician (6)
24 Slight gin cocktail on the rocks? (6)
26 Mark on a black beetle (6)
27 Holds up train during early hours (6)
28 Sound bites — a newscast's feature (4)

7

SPADEWORK

The eight unclued entries have something in common.

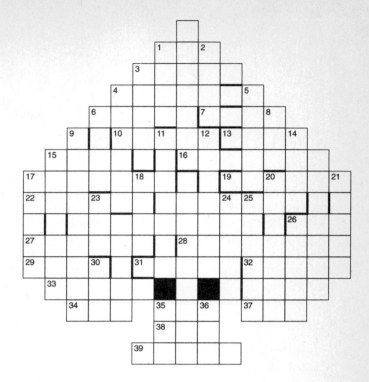

ACROSS

1 Bashful, but would be too self-assertive after turning up (3)
4 Maxwell's heart skipped beat (7)
6 The Greek leader in Yugoslavia recalled one (5)
7 More than one saying a woman is aboard ship (4)
10 Bruin stepped on the foot of beaver (5)
13 Nothing like penning Kilmer's original "Trees" (4)
15 Plant man (4)
16 Detective apprehends Miss Crane (7)
17 Rustic bum endlessly bellyaching? (7)
19 Frightened monk lies in comfort (6)
22 He combines uranium with saltpeter (6)
26 Essence of alien's story (3)
27 P.S.: Taking in large African animals (6)
28 Abstract muralist shows unselfish behavior (8)
29 Watch monkey's face appear (4)
31 Civil War general is behind me in fight (5)
32 Spreads cheer, very contrarily (5)
33 Wind heading west through Abilene, Kansas (5)
34 Tight end holds ball for kicker (3)
35 A Spanish viper (3)
37 Resident of Baltimore's sending a letter (3)
38 Leave ring of sticky stuff (3)
39 Quinine water served in goblet, on ice (5)

DOWN

1 Uppity sort gets turned on riding bull? (4)
2 Fix-up? Might result in canine cries (4)
3 A bit quiet, like a lobster? (5)
4 Bookkeeper initially filling in joint returns . . . to make you tremble (6)
5 Diminutive French word describing a building (5)
6 Z-Rock rejected nothing (4)
8 Runner is upset about finish in 10k (3)
9 Welcoming one detective coming in late (9)
11 Mr. Bunker takes the fifth — it's a matter of public record (7)
12 Multiply, perhaps . . . but become divorced, lacking love (7)
14 Foremost of second-graders is able to read (4)
15 Vandals harboring revolutionary feelings (7)
17 Scotsmen speak with these rabbis riding a coach (5)
18 Unjustified risk is troublesome (4)
20 Our slum is being ravaged by Wolfman? (7)
21 Judges remove page from thought-provoking manuscript (5)
23 Amount of profit going up (3)
24 Full-time nurse's last to wear blue (5)
25 Reagan sitting in the high chair? (6)
26 Banking arrangements in S&L reorganized to suppress error (5)
30 Chinese leader's mother love (3)
35 Silver ring in back (3)
36 Hawaiian food . . . semi-toxic? (3)

8
UPS & DOWNS

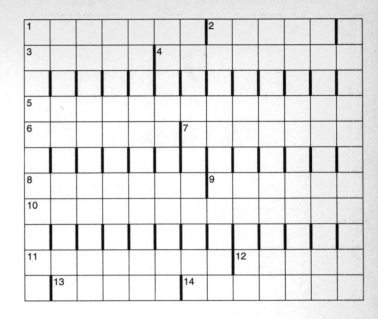

Across answers are to be entered normally. Downs, however, are to be entered sequentially, with the answer to Clue "a" starting in the square numbered 1 and reading down, and the remaining answers following down the first column, up the second, down the third, etc. Enumerations for the Downs have been withheld.

ACROSS

1 Legal document he had distorted (7)
2 Costner's holding back tears (5)
3 Heathen gets buried among monumental pillars? Just the opposite (5)
4 Prickly plant on meadow's periphery is not so easy to see (8)
5 City building where you'll get large frozen desserts coated in liquor (13, 2 wds.)
6 Put up with son and daughter, getting rushed (6)
7 Female sopranos outside New York repelled by timidity (7)
8 Humorous desire to pen outrageous gag (7)
9 Senator from the east keeps lady on hold (6)
10 Organ recital ending in *Duet in G*? It's thrilling (13, hyph.)
11 Lies in cots, if unmade (8)
12 Lofty nest in tree I read about (5)
13 Railroad guards are more exemplary (5)
14 Pulled us back up (7)

DOWN (& UP)

a Two women boarding a ship clumsily with lumber tool
b Expedition squad started on a distant island
c Rock opera written without hesitation by end of April
d Very tall mid-Westerner comes in to do the twist?
e Diary written by soldier at one open-air gallery
f Oppositionist stashes sculptures in box
g Piercing hole in "happy face" on front of garment
h From that place, you can go all around North Carolina
i Tree on lake's border arousing more passion
j Prostitute is rude to stranger
k Blessed derelict having nowhere to sleep
l Gab about excellent French poodle?
m Two knights on one horse following South American woman
n Frightfully aware, being captured by those people, roughly
o Car company accommodated by thin messenger
p Fine hole
q Light at first, like an eagle by the sea
r One tool set sent over for island carving
s More simply, see air polluted
t Dry run, getting help all around
u Offensive operator lives in Alaskan city
v Seductress about to be caught in unpardonable act
w Troll made the first move and got to first base

9

9 TO 5

Each answer is either 9 letters or 5 letters; clues for each length are given separately.

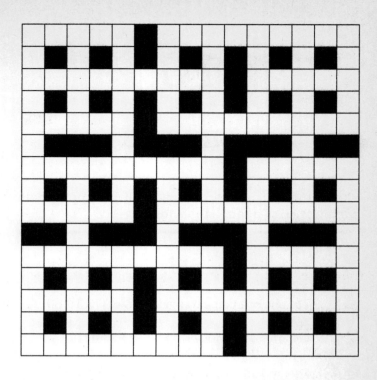

NINES

1 Cantor finds baby kangaroo living in ruins (2 wds.)

2 Keeping love in embrace and raising a ruckus

3 Doom the mother country?

4 Watched as I cried out loud

5 In eastern wharf bordering large lake . . . out of uniform?

6 Only taken in by one kind of raw deal

7 Janice absorbs small amount of color (2 wds.)

8 Gratuity is strangely appealing

9 Oaf wears small cap backwards as a baldness remedy

10 Chairperson is secure about free trade

11 Love poem deleted . . . too erotically inclined

12 Keep it up by itself, keeping on and on

13 Buyer turned up right before second drink

14 Agent, flyer, and mender

15 Ducks' velocity is boosted with injection of a pair of stimulants

16 One's hand is certain to catch one insect

FIVES

17 Letter indicates a desire

18 Sound of foreign car near rotary?

19 Ways to conceal messages in conservative poetry

20 Not bright to take measure of fabric

21 Overturned "D" at the right of Dutch flag

22 Cockney bets both ways to get advantages

23 Misguidedly says "Silver goggles"

24 Try deserting business in Asian river

25 Bottom of drain in need of cleaning

26 Wanderer gets turned on by bananas

27 Dirty words signifying nothing at high school

28 I don't broadcast rumor abroad (hyph.)

29 Ignoring piano, composer turned back

30 Bird having an argument that's one-sided?

31 Rock's upper surface, both ends

32 "Young at Heart" writer, down in defeat

10 ACROSTIC

First letters of answer words spell an appropriate modification of a familiar saying.

CLUES

A Saw parts of *E.T. The Extra-Terrestrial*? (5) (161 31 142 134 55)

B Spirit of one overcome by madness? (6) (73 19 60 168 57 118)

C "Love Party" — perfumer's latest scent (4) (174 77 135 148)

D We rose, repulsed by monster (8) (128 18 61 85 106 113 93 97)

E Coat necessary for winter in Detroit (4) (99 94 40 154)

F "I caught you adopting wild hippo" — bachelor assuming I may have a fear of snakes (11) (153 36 144 83 5 112 45 92 69 176 74)

G First and last, live in ultimate Biblical city (8) (87 121 10 109 181 101 49 42)

H Discussion covered in *Good Housekeeping* chart (5) (151 22 35 91 171)

I Russians help to capture southeast Asian (7) (75 138 166 43 17 82 105)

J Try to catch despot, having dined informally? (8, 3 wds.) (108 90 15 26 143 125 158 173)

K Long speech from one caught in traffic (6) (110 86 124 50 71 167)

L By its very nature, tête-à-tête will get to the heart of strange topic (9, 2 wds.) (156 4 48 98 179 132 81 28 21)

M Raise 51 feet (4) (64 104 12 51)

N Fat boy eats right (4) (175 145 127 66)

O Democratic stalwart under the influence? (7) (149 38 139 68 114 11 159)

P You can make this from iron, filled with a small amount of cream (8, hyph.) (70 136 79 46 16 165 146 178)

Q Drops off bridge from the other side (4) (24 180 117 27)

R Tackle with Santa's staff, not finished by midnight (6) (88 29 2 122 84 131)

S Settle an argument about city's prime doctor (8) (58 30 65 39 100 3 170 162)

T A vegetable or a nut (5) (116 182 126 14 62)

U New Zealanders embracing an organization of businesspersons (7) (32 23 41 107 133 119 157)

V Boys were misbehaving — they're raised by skeptics (8) (183 111 129 152 59 67 1 33)

W Believe apartment has capacity for 200 people, ultimately (6) (56 163 137 96 34 102)

X Again, use cooked celery to garnish piece of chicken (7) (140 52 120 72 177 6 78)

Y Restless one has your stocking cap, at first (5) (9 164 44 89 155)

Z Country has oil, reportedly (6) (8 20 47 80 95 160)

AA Domestic uses garden tool to get me angry (8) (103 13 147 37 130 76 53 172)

BB Roughly a half-score behold a musical rendition (9, 2 wds.) (54 123 169 150 115 141 63 25 7)

1V	2R		3S	4L	5F	6X	7BB	8Z	9Y	10G	11O		12M	13AA	14T		15J	16P	17I		18D	19B
20Z	21L	22H		23U	24Q		25BB	26J	27Q	28L		29R	30S	31A	32U	33V		34W	35H	36F	37AA	38O
	39S	40E		41U	42G	43I	44Y	45F		46P	47Z		48L	49G	50K	51M	52X	53AA		54BB	55A	56W
57B		58S	59V		60B	61D	62T	63BB	64M	65S		66N	67V	68O	69F	70P	71K	72X		73B	74F	75I
	76AA		77C	78X	79P	80Z	81L	82I	83F	84R	85D		86K	87G		88R	89Y	90J		91H	92F	93D
94E	95Z	96W		97D	98L	99E	100S	101G		102W	103AA	104M	105I		106D	107U	108J		109G		110K	111V
112F	113D	114O	115BB	116T	117Q	118B		119U	120X	121G	122R		123BB	124K	125J	126T	127N		128D	129V		130AA	131R
132L	133U	134A		135C	136P		137W	138I	139O	140X	141BB	142A		143J	144F	145N	146P		147AA	148C		149O
150BB	151H	152V	153F	154E	155Y		156L	157U		158J		159O	160Z	161A	162S	163W	164Y	165P	166I	167K		168B
169BB		170S	171H	172AA		173J	174C	175N	176F	177X	178P		179L	180Q	181G	182T	183V					

11
26 SIXES

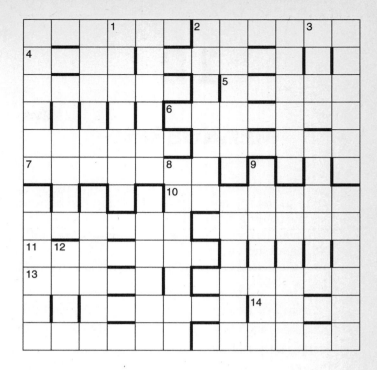

Clues to the 26 6-letter words in this puzzle are given out of sequence and are designated by letter. In each case, this letter belongs to the answer, but is not accounted for in the clue's wordplay.

ACROSS

4 River in Spain, or in the Bronx? (4)
5 With a bit of money, king's employee gives help from above (5)
6 After start of Fireman's Ball, I had sampling of snack bars (7)
7 Runner is cycling in kimonos (7)
10 Damn dogs caught by expert (7)
11 Pieces of rope run through bleachers (7)
13 Take possession of northern port (5)
14 Who's looking to acquire capital? (4)

DOWN

1 Dances may reveal largely flagrant libido (7)
2 Rustic young reporter from the south covers source of crude oil spill (7)
3 Smack with this! (4)
8 Kids had rewritten mourners' prayer (7)
9 Crossed through south, nonstop, to return formal wear (7)
12 Bug eats piece of meat from pack (4)

SIXES

a Warm object used when playing around street
b Move up and down in reel
c A cheapskate's backless smock
d Lady wears smile to show confusion?
e All but team's anchor run on the level
f Gnarled trees rot
g Intelligent Englishman has an aspiration
h Princess is upset over sulphur in hair dyes
i Keys rented aboard ship
j Kids love women
k Use the key of C after Spaniard's opening number about incipient love
l Warns of a change in rates
m Disciplinarian's irrational ardor
n Smart person's deceptive guise
o News staffer tried broadcasting
p Ostentatious show is cut
q Boor eats a kind of fruit
r Eliminates cushions
s Most mature couple from Richmond to get amorous
t Fools and their money?
u Be flirtatious two ways
v It's a horse . . . little wonder
w That is most extensive
x Prepared to take off, even with ace aboard
y Ignoring the odds bookmaker'd approved
z Impudent bachelor approaching from below

12

MEANDERING

After solving, find an appropriate 10-word song lyric, beginning in the top square and ending in the bottom square, by tracing a meandering path through the diagram from letter to letter (never moving diagonally or crossing a black bar).

ACROSS

2 Sampling of tresses, hairpiece or small switch (4)
6 Laughter that's boundless, echoed? (4, hyph.)
9 Composer pinching rear of George Sand (5)
13 With one word, train son to juggle fruits (11)
16 Captured by formerly silent person, I cry (7)
17 Hedonists recalled burying horse in trench (6)
21 Mobs fight to be in possession of recordings (6)
22 A leader in trade started west to river area (5)
24 Dee hurried back for medicinal plant (4)
25 Little yellow flower (4)
26 Nothing bad until the finale (6)
28 Child, long repulsed by meat (6)
31 Feels contempt for Democrat, said to worry officeholders (8)
32 Leave bubble gum (3)
34 Busy with college musicfest (5)
35 Musical instrument in band rang out (5)
37 Broadway awards? Outwardly, they're mere trinkets (4)
41 See Mother look around in powder room? (8)
45 Heats dressing, previously stews (7)
47 Bony old pirate (6)
48 Freshly covered in cellophane wrap (4)
49 Some carrot salad turns bad (4)
50 Writing in *Times* about end of the strike (4)
51 Do-nothing hayseed returned the old thing (9)

DOWN

1 In short, he mimicked others (4)
2 Set up a ball bearing with cloth (5)
3 Become Polish? (3)
4 Long throw loses power (4)
5 Money gain overcomes loss (4)
7 Do I exist, friend? (3)
8 Mountain in central Pennsylvania (3)
9 Putting up with bad groin wound (8)
10 Gives a shiny coating to English automobile (7)
11 Stick around, poor lady — it's a wicked thing (6)
12 My family is sheltered by unusually shy wench (5)
14 Amid cheers, there's agreement from the German princes (6)
15 One involved in rock cutting (6)
18 Man spots a Ford model and makes an acrobatic maneuver (9)
19 Can't do much to advertise *Colonist's World*? (6)
20 Chocolate (about a cup) and a doughnut (5)
23 Address for a noble is somewhat ludicrous (3)
27 Dog's tail in trap (3)
28 Aperitif consumed by drunk, I reckon (3)
29 New York club occupied by the Spanish rustics (7)
30 Cheer one just before the end of race (6)
33 Fancy talk about leader of nation (6)
36 Old Mexican sleuth on the trail of a crooked character (5)
38 I turned east, making a curve (4)
39 Yard bird's holler (4)
40 Fringe on surfboard is irrational (4)
42 Fur dealer in a shop with no foundation (5)
43 My wild hogs (4)
44 Moving nonstop in wine region (4)
46 Team's opener . . . a scoreless tie, moreover? (3)

13
BIG DEAL

Don't be misled by the strange numbering in the diagram. Some of the numbers are themselves the clues to the otherwise unclued entries, all members of the same set (though not all members of the same set).

2	4	14	5		8	10	12	20	21	23	24
25						13		26			
27				28				29			
30				31				32			
	9		1			33					
34	35			7							
6				3					19	17	
36		37		38	39		22	40			
41			42		18						
	15					16		43			
44				45							
11					46						

ACROSS

2 Necessary bit of tartrate in test tube (5)
6 Slight inclination (4)
10 Go downhill, as in bed (5)
25 Boss, involved in game, to read ahead? (8)
26 Stick around — I will come back with couturier (4)
27 Crossing borders, man halts (5)
28 Spot 100 parrots? (3)
29 Single old lady in New York (4)
30 Jelly dish in a small photo (5)
31 Carolinian has pieces of leather (7, 2 wds.)
33 Singer prepared for audition (5)
34 Small light switches in Asian nation (5)
36 Running around with Grant? (3)
37 Initially locked into gridlock, heed the traffic signal (5)
40 Part of computer set (3)
41 Replacing sin (4)
42 Prompt by quoting a line . . . (3)
44 . . . a line from Meyerbeer opera (4)
45 Bands of rats running around tree from the other side (7)
46 Cover a radio station that plays only "gangsta" music? (4)

DOWN

4 Essentially, Bird is center for the Celtics (5)
5 Hoping not to need good painkiller (7)
12 To hear in court vestibule beyond the entrance (4)
15 Party time period (3)
20 Bother operator following commercial (3)
21 *Rocky II* needs to be without a specific date (7, 2 wds.)
23 To model topless around Ohio city (6)
24 Ironically, poet is talking (5)
25 Puts up the money to package 50 dramas (5)
32 German man and woman run (4)
33 Ultimately, viewer likely to become engrossed (4)
35 The old white wood (3)
37 First Lady seen during the French reception (5)
38 Silence stifles pair of ultraliberals in prison camp (5)
39 *Middle Man* sculpture (5)
40 Might pass someone with debts (5)
43 "H" as in "Hoffmann"? (3)

14

IN ALL DIRECTIONS

Each answer begins in the appropriate square and reads in a straight line in one of the eight main compass directions. Letters around the diagram's border will reveal some suitable words; not all the border squares will be used, however.

CLUES

1 Ensconced in insane asylum, with much comfort (4)
2 Associate with fattest member of family tree (4)
3 Formerly on cable, after central characters have been eliminated (5)
4 Certain right acquired by petition (4)
5 River bend . . . I will circle this mark! (6)
6 Run from Bailey (4)
7 Enjoyment one gets, at first, around animals (5)
7 Portion of Grofé's suite rendered by band crossing the field (4)
8 Italian fair in bay area (5)
9 One page — editor made copies? (4)
10 Enter forcefully and vie to get a new position (6)
11 Happy when my banks fail? (5)
12 Highest point occupied by unknown islanders of Britain (4)
13 Italian man's autograph, as an alternative (6)
14 Overture begun with organ in a Broadway musical (6)
15 Briefly sees demons suppressed by unmarried people without sin (8)
16 Barbarian puts silver in reserve (6)
17 Pound on sweetheart (5)
18 Opposed to recall of South American minister (6)
19 He left a piece of lead underground (4)
20 Father's getting married in grassy region (6)
20 Dances with president, for example (6)
21 Riding public transportation, daughter begins to blossom (4)
22 Learns of the woman's checking account being opened (5)
23 Youngster nearly completed one beef dish (5)

24 Insignificant one beheaded tramp down in New York (6)
24 Dissolute count joins nurse in prayer (7)
25 Group of soldiers flipping the bird, incidentally (5)
26 New TV network carries nothing immediately after (4)
27 Sound made by wheel at rear of German car (5)
28 Who's going topless? The King's friend? Hallelujah! (7)
29 Wearing hat, leader of expedition told stories (4)
30 Opposite sex's clothing worn by monster (6)
31 Top meal, after the start (5)
32 Never-ending party on one island (4)
33 "Smack" is synonymous with this! (4)
33 A bit crazy, packing a quantity of cocaine in knapsack (6)
34 Praise comes back twofold (4)
35 Singer, in this manner, belted rap number (7)
36 Reportedly recognize a boatman (4)
37 Serpent was repulsive (5)
38 E.g., Mexican-American man's fear (8)
39 Rod Serling's initial depression (4)
40 Accuse one male snitch (7)
40 Thin paper, excluding the first edition (5)
41 Mender is set again to make a comeback (6)
42 Almost everything . . . then it's settled (4)
42 Eager to eat egg from duck (5)
43 Let "a little bit o' luck" make things simpler (5)
44 At the conclusion, priest then replaced tithed amount (5)

15

5 x 5

The "quotation" in this puzzle is actually a sequence of five additional cryptic clues (separated by three consecutive black squares). The answers to these five clues are 5-letter words that, in order, form a word square.

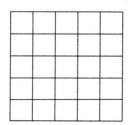

CLUES

A Spy stops short, conceals small brush (5)
(9 23 111 129 116)

B Stimulant poured into cup (5)
(91 11 134 32 138)

C One forbidding flag (6)
(183 74 154 96 103 170)

D Fashion designer's name on envelope (6)
(163 54 173 17 145 28)

E Being more cheerful, talk foolishly (7)
(98 85 39 65 76 106 5)

F Foremost of chain stands before willowy mountaineer (7) (49 159 20 79 136 93 151)

G Soft bed, quite stylish (7)
(156 109 68 177 35 130 15)

H Almost nude, gets all mixed up (7)
(89 137 26 144 117 40 94)

I Pope broadcasting during bishop's final argument (7) (81 72 13 149 114 44 168)

J Bigot describes last bit in burlesque, "risqué in the extreme" (7) (142 123 161 52 21 61 97)

K Sitting in cedar tree, leaning back, I used the CB (7) (107 127 6 124 43 181 57)

L Circling court, tennis star makes a decision (7) (176 148 18 42 100 104 69)

M Source of shade, otherwise dark (7)
(121 55 152 112 175 64 70)

N Held to be trite, without a trace of novelty (8) (48 165 63 33 75 90 184 19)

O Disciple rose to take backward look (8)
(53 47 166 125 157 12 120 178)

P Funny — Mr. Nelson sounds suicidal (8)
(128 36 87 58 101 164 3 80)

Q In all likelihood, cop will be stuck in bottom of deep well (8) (84 185 169 14 99 131 158 8)

R In a movie, a fish is caught by appropriate weapon (11, 3 wds.) (45 78 140 118 59 110 66 30 147 133 1)

S A certain glow may please when lady is bathed in it (11) (41 4 119 143 51 82 102 27 155 174 162)

T Poet to score grass in western spread (11, 2 wds.) (83 180 31 172 139 10 113 146 132 25 73)

U South American guitarist playing for a group of stars (11) (16 141 29 2 122 37 179 46 88 150 62)

V Paint fellows with true character (11)
(71 95 182 38 160 22 60 108 86 56 126)

W Arguments from nomads in Canada, initially discussing alliances (13) (34 171 67 105 7 50 92 135 115 167 153 24 77)

16 ROTATIONS

Each answer is to be entered with its letters rotated; thus, the answer WORD would appear as ORDW, RDWO, or DWOR.

ACROSS

1 We're told of quest to acquire ornamental disk (6)
5 Give payment to landlord taking train (6)
10 Race halfway completed in bad weather (4)
12 Center of poorly lit back street (5)
13 Foreign nation that's not shut up? (5)
14 Plundering in Chile's capital squelched by South American monarch (7)
15 Altered the facts in fish-catching stories (7)
17 Planned for airplane to carry *Chronicle*'s lead editor (9)
18 Man leaves romance novel in pupil's coat (6)
20 Leader shows where Y is? (4)
23 Men discovered turning on gas (4)
25 Texas city passed on returning between terminals (6)
27 Not going straight in gets toe broken (9)
32 Wild French caper (7)
33 Boy runs in with club — it doesn't matter who (7)
34 Communist Party repulsed stranger (5)
35 Packs two bombs aboard ship (5)
36 Trick uses hot wax coating (4)
37 Cheap little devil wearing blue (6)
38 Tell bishop after commencement (6)

DOWN

1 Worldwide organization described by saintly composer (6)
2 I moved to the center of car in rockpile (5)
3 *No, No, Nanette*'s lead character has a good figure (7)
4 Robinson and Simpson wearing bracelets (9)
5 California baseball team's dog (6)
6 In hangar, you'll find normal astronaut (7)
7 Mountains with crests at the center (5)
8 Lady in bed with young stud? (4)
9 Basketball star appearing in *Psycho* remake (6)
11 Angered from buggy ride (4)
16 It's upsetting to excellent *Glamour* photographer (9)
19 Pine boards given a finish by female senior (7)
21 Ten-time winner's back in step for dance (7, 2 wds.)
22 Mawkish gentleman not in bed by end of day (6)
24 Take someone to see *King and I* sent up — a bit of parody (6)
26 Was very fond of tot carrying rock (6)
28 Turn back to somebody (5)
29 No name, nevertheless (4)
30 Member of regiment assumes leader was informed (5)
31 Resident in condominium observes crowds (4)

17

EIGHTSOME REELS

Each answer is 8 letters long. These letters are to be entered in the eight spaces surrounding (but not including) the corresponding numbered space. Each answer may read clockwise or counterclockwise and may begin in any of the eight spaces.

CLUES

1 Mark has to go cold turkey, almost (2 wds.)
2 Certain to be buried among large amounts of shavings
3 *Caine*'s captain has to look around for wiper
4 Caterer provides dinner to accommodate 51
5 Drove one mile, then begged to take train
6 Eastern holy man overwhelmed by stacks of letters
7 Eccentric idolater made adjustments
8 Tough guy keeps crude oil in Navaho dwelling
9 Prostitute's friend claims it to be a place to get drugs
10 Criminal stealing some desserts
11 Save about 500 copies in foreign city

12 Big blasts from faulty magnetos
13 Kiss and hug southern copper after hours
14 Interpreter's mother caught by monster
15 Team has woman stifled
16 Bum intimate with novice
17 Members of laid-back combo's outrivaled a skilled musician
18 Agree with the destruction of money?
19 Poem, "Time Runs Thru Paradise" (2 wds.)
20 Gift for Queen Elizabeth, in the near future
21 Suitable to wear khaki pants in warm winds
22 Tree fixed by emergency treatment (2 wds.)
23 Family member in appliance store
24 One male spy conceals a true sacrifice
25 Prepare to shoot at eggs of bird
26 Female lover takes flight with torch
27 Bells ring halfway through visit
28 Magnificent canyon seen by half of us
29 First exam during which I drink
30 Very loudly, tabloid enters petition for vote
31 Silly little ones leave casts?
32 Under attack, I see . . . perhaps good in bed?
33 Flower got from the Spanish salesperson
34 Raillery about one's railing?
35 Defamatory writer is living in Long Island region
36 In the UK, make small hole in which one man lives
37 More than one top that is spinning, framed by sticks
38 Gain reforms after overly contrived political plan
39 Island baseball team consumed by true enthusiasm
40 Close to agreement, returned for a drink

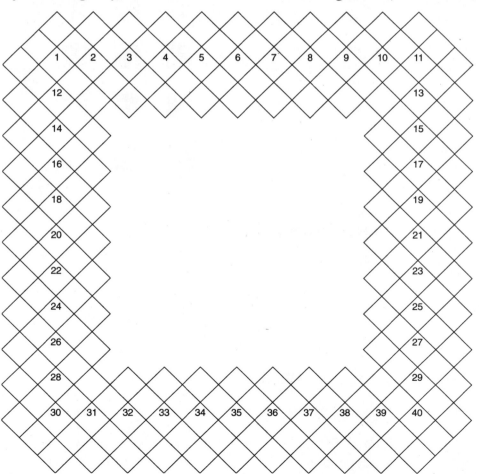

18 TRIPLETS

Clues are given in sets of three, the answers to each threesome occupying the same place in the three diagrams, although not necessarily respectively.

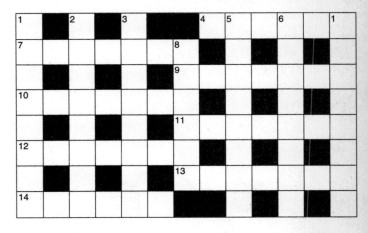

ACROSS

4 Perhaps the Siamese eat a condiment (6)

Set fire to headquarters of Scottish orthodox churches (6)

Scrape damaged typewriter key (6)

7 Perpetual fool filled with playful glee (7)

Surpass rates of speed maintained by eastern pair? (7)

Wins the affection of Ed Asner, somehow (7)

9 Blended date-nut fruitcake (7)

Tenor, in sumptuous surroundings, perversely rejoiced (7)

Inquires about volume, *The Essence of Anita Loos* (7)

10 Something really funny in excavation in Massachusetts city (7)

Strange quality of two Democrats boarding a ship (7)

Team taking note of last part of Einstein's formula? (7)

11 Don't sailors cross in a junk? (7)

Mobile home (?) in which a group of doctors maintains a place to experiment (7)

Some swimmers eagerly plunge into the water (7)

12 Painting red number in boat (7)

Defensive wall of great size hindering battle (7)

"I am almost laughing" in Spanish or Portuguese (7)

13 Continues to talk about legal matter in speech (7)

Network claims First Lady was very sorry (7)

End of *Week in Rock* featured in *Saturday Night Live* — it's good for a breather (7)

14 Whichever one is overcome by anesthetic (6)

Talk-show host reveals what's at the heart of scandal in roadside stopover (6)

Wearing corset, stripper finally goes off (6)

DOWN

1 Devotion to pleasure revealed in Sondheim medley (8)

Adequate piece of poplin-like black fur (8)

Studies about 500 male auburn-haired people (8)

2 Move along, carrying large club (8)

One of 10 children in France, of course, started up to leave (8)

Worshipper's marriage vow, subsequently (8)

3 A quiet little desire (8)

Lower number finally seen in die (8)

Classification of tariff on oil originally done by me (8)

5 One turning back, not giving name, is a rabblerouser (8)

Social organization's recalled commotion in mixer (8, 2 wds.)

Verse describing head of the family of Russian statesman (8)

6 Being opposed to the gist of tragedy always repulsed dramatist (8)

Went back along to find wagon overturned in tall grass (8)

Glance at questions — they may conceal robbers' identities (8, 2 wds.)

8 Conclusion of jamboree . . . a musicfest is relaxing (6)

Singer-songwriter used a kazoo at the bridge (6)

Talks with sons about mountain (6)

19 ACROSTIC

Though technically, it's not, since the initial letters in the word list don't spell anything . . . which may be as frustrating as the events described in the quote.

CLUES

A Call "time" after start of pole vault (5)
(132 90 58 169 68)

B Dancing until dark (5) (9 123 84 151 19)

C Travels with members of the football team (5)
(27 75 118 108 166)

D Support routine maintained by Catholic Church (6)
(173 43 85 50 87 147)

E Mixed-up myth of irreparable character? (6)
(79 32 55 99 111 59)

F Encountered brick carrier, in a way (6)
(104 72 11 161 138 110)

G Tungsten rings? Uh-oh! (6)
(120 179 17 182 31 136)

H Tenant, holding center of key, to come back in (7)
(174 36 2 47 146 105 23)

I Very different tranquilizer (7)
(93 117 28 80 121 40 181)

J Like an orphan, if one gets caught in shower (7)
(165 95 77 41 144 37 81)

K Swedish man pursuing town's thieves (8)
(97 69 8 65 133 56 157 25)

L Tied up alien repulsed by Eric (8)
(178 53 14 125 164 29 60 153)

M Country gent ultimately welcome as well (8)
(149 88 129 49 94 13 18 141)

N Amount that can make you smooth (8)
(160 112 66 134 44 126 102 20)

O Some nobles used explosive to capture game (9)
(73 142 83 39 170 6 176 158 128)

P All apparel is said to be in an unspecified location (9)
(3 24 96 115 76 156 100 62 10)

Q Makes one review New York State before the masses (11)
(114 1 57 124 150 140 106 52 33 162 177)

R Incarceration of boy and me described by Mark (12)
(42 184 167 152 109 98 21 101 70 82 145 127)

S Man without a topic pertaining to numbers (12)
(74 172 45 12 148 130 89 7 154 116 61 35)

T Dolt gets in, drinks a couple with actor (13, 2 wds.)
(22 91 15 163 5 131 103 67 155 139 46 183 54)

U City vehicle in which guides left, taking tip from town crier (13, 2 wds.) (63 38 171 113 135 78 26 159 86 180 71 122 51)

V I lead in play (one-act), *In Place of Chaos* . . . had reflective song (13, hyph.) (34 4 143 168 119 48 92 16 107 175 30 64 137)

1	2	3		4	5	6		7	8	9	10		11	12	13	14		15		16	17	18
19		20	21		22	23	24	25	26	27	28	29	30		31	32	33	34	35	36	37	
38	39	40		41	42	43	44	45		46	47	48		49		50	51	52	53	54		55
56	57	58		59	60	61	62	63		64	65	66		67	68	69	70	71	72	73		74
75		76	77	78	79		80	81	82		83	84	85	86		87	88	89	90	91	92	93
	94	95	96	97	98		99	100	101		102	103	104	105		106	107		108	109	110	
111	112	113		114	115	116	117	118	119		120	121	122	123		124	125	126	127		128	129
130	131		132	133	134	135		136	137	138	139	140	141		142	143		144	145		146	147
148		149	150	151	152	153		154		155	156	157	158	159		160	161	162		163	164	165
166	167	168	169	170	171		172	173	174	175	176	177		178	179	180		181	182	183	184	

20

THEME & VARIATIONS

Nine entries are unclued. These include three words (A, B, and C), a familiar trio. Each Theme Word has two Variations — words related to it in some way (a different way for each Theme Word).

ACROSS

2 Scratch around a bit to find cannon (6)
7 Six foreign airline endorsements (5)
12 Fly perched on the head of tailless little dog (5, hyph.)
14 Least sparkling diamond — Frenchwoman's wearing it (7)
16 Before a successor is announced (3)
17 Variation on Theme Word A (4)
18 A piece of cheese eaten by gorilla quickly (5)
19 Pair besieged by trouble for just over four weeks (5)
20 Tropical flower . . . might be a big one (7)
21 Variation on Theme Word B (6)
22 Storage areas help to keep interest low (5)
26 Outspoken Florida athletes' spats (7)
29 Before striking the head of scholar (5)
30 Doctor needs new porcelainware (7)
33 California region features a waterfall (8)
35 Stay with one in unmade bed (4)
36 Recognized an antelope by its call (4)
38 Variation on Theme Word B (7)
39 Clever bit about woman (6)
40 Theme Word B (6)
42 Time oven needs to get, ultimately, very warm (6)
43 Edging away from lurching child (6)
44 Letter indicates daughter running late (5)
45 The French monarch has a plumbing problem (7)

DOWN

1 In conclusion, Congress' top orators do it (5)
2 Use a computer to adjust mileage, adopting odometer's limitations (5)
3 Before the finale, talk-show host takes in excellent stage presentation (5)
4 Obstacle I study in river (7)
5 A Dalmatian's head has small spots (3)
6 Reins may get all tangled up (5)
8 One man mails taxes (7)
9 A scene is restaged in a spirited session? (6)
10 For example, #102 in computer code (5)
11 Sons framing wood cuts of a sort (8)
13 Variation on Theme Word A (4)
15 Variation on Theme Word C (6)
20 Variation on Theme Word C (8, 2 wds.)
22 Bags or cans (5)
23 I have no problem with Scott's story (7)
24 One type of football pass following goal . . . no go (7)
25 Theme Word A (5)
27 Crafty bowman appears without hesitation (4)
28 Washington athlete drinks rum around end of game (7)
31 Stamp first letter in delivery, that is (3)
32 All points bulletin (4)
34 At the beginning, four fish (5)
35 Theme Word C (5)
37 Direction given my group on street (4)
40 Leader of underworld entering signature at the top and bottom of petition (3)
41 Machine displays the letter X (3)

21 RUNAROUND

The answer to each clue begins in the appropriate square and continues in a straight line up, down, left, or right. Many answers run off one edge of the diagram and continue at the opposite edge, so imagine the grid to be toroidal. Each letter is used exactly twice.

CLUES

1 Rubble in layer overturned by misguided knight (6)
2 Place to have a spat inside, repulsing members of the household (6)
3 Apprehend Greek sailor (4)
4 Silver money, $100 short (3)
5 Neat pilot (5)
6 One to inquire about forger's next-to-last copy (5)
7 Ammunition chest is then coated with tin (7)
8 Record player taken by us during a break (7)
9 Gay Nineties genius (8)
10 Chinese book shows heroin mixed into cake frosting (6, 2 wds.)
11 A little change is somewhat rudimentary (4)
12 What you believe about rug that's burned (8)
13 Country singer in after the first half (4)
14 A bunch of people go in Scotland (4)
15 Flower worn by a queen got from Arabs (6)
16 Forceful opening from Hendrix song not so captivating as performed by me (8)
17 Concerning planes in Korea, mostly heading west (4)
18 Mideast group is beginning to resent an Ivy League team (8)
19 Abridged tearjerker about sailor somewhere in Canada (7)
20 Yes, eccentric has collected 2,000 awards (5)
21 Northern boy, not entirely sincere (6)
22 Seven performing seals beginning to sing — it's something to see (6)
23 It's crucial for ladies to wear green (5)
24 Furniture of the French kings (5)
25 Imperiled woman moving up a row (7)
25 Cat turned up with mother (4)
26 I retracted advertisements with 20% taken off home of medium structure (12)
27 Racer, one who pulls back, adopting royal name (12, hyph.)

28 In Germany, I will conceal true desire (4)
29 Counter transaction has good man held up (6)
30 Woman would be angry with me if time were a factor (6)
30 West Virginia finally gets to the heart of me (3)
31 Steal into kitchen imperceptibly (3)
32 It's caught up in head-cord that can be broken (12)
33 Sex drive, unencumbered by marriage vow? That's freedom (3)
34 Just by eating live ladybug's head (6)
35 Middle of ceiling's almost straight (6)
36 Actor in *Casablanca* and *Stormy Weather* (5)
37 Pair of legislators written about in various releases (8)
37 Ambassadors always holding back (6)
38 Hint: copper kettle's bottom (3)
39 Sequence of musical notes went on and on (6)
40 Prosecutors turning blue (3)
40 Head of government overwhelmed by evil omen (4)
41 Georgia woman's legs (4)
42 Completely fill an Indonesian dish (4)
43 Sacred feature of XXVIIth Olympics (4)
44 Midwesterner was undone in a little bit (5)
45 Norm initially wears reversible cover (4)
46 Winged one from Transylvania (3)
47 Every teacher has it (4)
48 Letters to take to the auditor (4)

22

RIDDLE ME THIS

Each answer is to be entered with one letter omitted, as reflected by the wordplay in the clues. Write this omitted letter on the corresponding dash(es) below to spell a poser.

ACROSS

 1 Discard small hat (5)
 4 Mobbism gets ugly after introduction of terrible explosives (9, 2 wds.)
10 Fellows I met at sea during the same period (8)
11 Arctic diver has a piece of latex to prevent leakage (5)
12 Secretary has to change the name (5)
13 In a groggy way, yowl uncontrollably about a magic land (7)
14 Conservative goddess of peace, Egyptian (7)
16 I'm captivated by spinning device in airplane (8)
17 Composer in seedy dive (5)
18 500 feet off . . . one vessel's bow is about 100 off (9)
20 End of race is horse's comeback, to make a long story short (9)
24 Pulled in our direction? (5)
26 Tip of knife stuck in neck — gee, it's frightening (8)
28 The German has encountered a goddess (7)
31 It takes a long time to support a math class (7)
32 Lifesaver given to flying ace in sea (5)
33 One who angers the boss, at times? (5)
34 He crosses the line in one hour, in more elegant surroundings (8)
35 Northern rebel surely attains victory with agitation (9)
36 Fighter in dirty sneakers (5)

DOWN

 1 Man in San Francisco . . . he's looking rather blue (5)
 2 Speed endlessly, as the poets say, through town (8)
 3 Small chickens live among insects (7)
 4 In a contrary way, I've been tagged as shy (5)
 5 I'm in favor of primary education — it's better (7)
 6 Planned to fill cheese with a form of chewy chocolate (7)
 7 Stubborn fellow comprehends "crooked line" gag (6)
 8 Middle lines in *Times* (5)
 9 Floppy disk #6-1000 features "Year in Sport" (9)
14 Tinted egg, Easter's biggest, stored in low temperature (7)
15 Landlord sometimes in covert operation (7)
16 It's used to check everything else before storm (9)
19 They're engaged in a struggle, I can see (8)
21 Comic troupe with wings, in the end (7)
22 Raising money in Italy, detective has to gamble (7)
23 Short legend about church is lacking in detail (7)
25 Someone crying . . . could be smaller? (6)
27 Go along with gear shifts (5)
29 Last bit of paint — unspecified amount of yellow-brown (5)
30 Make long (5)

| 6D | 33A | 10A | 16A | 4A | 32A | 16D | 1A | 30D | 13A | 9D | 18A | 5D | 28A | 17A | 30D | 11A |

| 14D | 35A | 34A | 21D | 29D | 36A | 1A | 24A | 25D | 1D | 20A | 7D | 31A | 8D | 6D | 35A | 1D |

| 2D | 4D | 3D | 27D | 14A | 25D | 10A | 31A | 26A | 32A | 24A | 17A | 36A | 22D | 4A | 15D | 19D |

| 13A | 23D | 34A | 19D | 26A | 14D | 21D | 16A | 2D | 18A | 16D | 23D | 28A | 1A | 29D | 8D | 17A |

| 27D | 11A | 33A | 14A | 9D | 12A | 4A | 4D |

?

23

EVERYTHING IN ITS PLACE

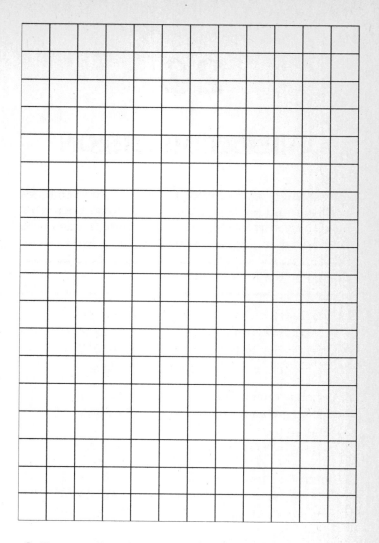

This puzzle is to be solved as a diagramless, with placement of numbers and black bars (and several black squares) to be determined by the solver. As a help, the four unclued answers will appear in their relative positions in the diagram and are hints to its general shape.

ACROSS

1 Heroin stashed in bottle in case head of DEA's to put a value on "sugar" (12)
11 Goes on links for sport, initially! (5)
13 German woman took cover outside L.A. (5)
15 Unless you've just begun, keep informed (6)
16 Entrance opened for court physician (6)
17 Getting last bit of smoke from butt turned disastrous (6)
18 *See instructions* (4)
19 I'm surprised about a true swearword (4)
20 Old king works with flowers (8)
22 Rube traveling over in Berlin (4)
25 Writer has trouble describing novel's lead character (7)
28 *See instructions* (4)
31 Resistance is helpful in incursions (5)
32 Woman of the night? (3)
33 Get access to government file (5)
34 *See instructions* (3)
36 Fragment of sidewalk drops on the grass (3)
37 Carving in grease-gun seen from the other side (8)
39 Tip O'Neill's irrational number (10)
41 Woman cooked meals (5)
44 Donkey's last, awfully low outcry (4)
46 Benefit from rice drink (4)
47 *Heart of Our Endless Emptiness* penned by grizzly French writer (8)
48 Perversely show scorn after finally eating salad fixings (6)
50 Hire delinquent gang to infiltrate east end (6)
51+52+53 Criminal steals pendant (6)

DOWN

1 Aware of sports . . . all the better to get in shape? (9)
2 Coin from Israel's marketplace (5)
3 Baloney consumed in turn (6)
4 Captain to take poison just before the end (5)
5 Commit murder twice in workplace (6)
6 Singers' Club band . . . striking people? (8)
7 Wild dog beginning to dig hole (5)
8 Famous admiral can't get over haystack (4)
9 Chorus members joining recital to sing (5)
10 In repair class, every second counts (5)
12 Flatterer won't, when in possession of forged copy (9)
14 They get spotted doing somersault after party (6)
21 Working with my team during start of game (5)
23 Angle for bluefish (?), gaining velocity (5)
24 Yes, yes — stealing uranium is the work of a villain (7)
26 Incendiary material catches ally in war zone (6)
27 Shed light on fabric (5)
29 Some schoolboys went back with lots of information (5)
30 Stagehand's endless complaint (4)
34 Lamb to eat piece of zucchini offered by fair lady (5)
35 Performing in fancy Disney movie (8, 2 wds.)
38 Jungle beast almost devours everything back in cultivated area (7)
40 *See instructions* (8, 2 wds.)
41 To cry loudly . . . er . . . would make this serious (3)
42 They have wool coats nearly stitched up (4)
43 Five Gaelic poems (5)
45 Overcooked last piece of chicken in Reynolds wrap? (5)
49 Museum supporter is almost asleep, tossing and turning (5)

24

DIVISION DIVERSION

The diagram is divided into 16 sections, each consisting of a numbered square and the eight squares immediately surrounding it. The answer to each clue is to be entered across or down, with at least one of its letters in the correspondingly numbered section. Answer lengths have been withheld.

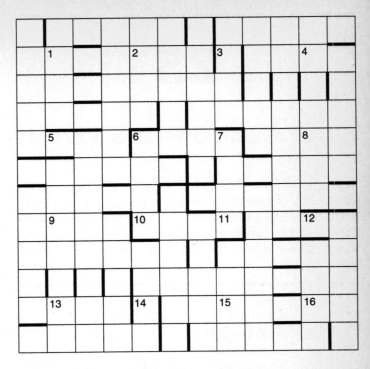

CLUES

1 Proscription, among other things, in European land
Chicago player holding end of baseball bat
Mr. French, when working for bricklayer

2 Coach prematurely ended old song
Sign that shows me wearing large woman's underwear
Responsibility that we'll pay for?

3 Returned some merchandise, including liqueur
Give a new name to alien pictured in tabloid
Without a hint of machismo, yield to American demoness

4 Highest degree revoked after English test
Access to underground spy outside a hospital
007's boss demands disguises

5 Wrongly handles westbound vessel in its milieu?
Artesian well erected in April, for years and years?
Vagrants discovered instruments

6 By crossing ravine, a river is seen
Raymond Knight's announcing track athletes
Conceited author in front

7 Aces shuffled into pack
Understand Greek well enough
Arabs in US said to be violent

8 Fatalities from low-grade food laced with heroin
Former prostitute takes one way off the street? (2 wds.)
Jewels friend set into rings

9 Boldness seen in a cheater's face during examination (final in trigonometry)
Beat-up old car . . . one comes in with it
Boy, after lunch, doffing coat, proves to be naked

10 Bit of rye added to iced rum drink
Member of the service back in camp after "Taps"?
Word from the text of "Silver Bells"

11 Participate in a sport in a stadium
I'm a green and orange bug
Coward in a work of fiction, without vice

12 Impersonator begins a performance
Messengers find me in shady glen
Cast iron's something used to make varnish

13 Throw beef
Singer has everything needed to build a Model T
Ready misses beamed

14 Old advertisement about appliance company
Mangled body buried in leaves and . . . Cheerios?
Fond of rocking, fall asleep (2 wds.)

15 Bet $1,000 on what a pacer might do
Sol would make it firmly but casually
Tried to win without a big dictionary

16 They change color, swirling red with yellow and a hint of silver
Began associating with independent movie director
Odd characters in Greene's clan

25

IT COULD BE VERSE

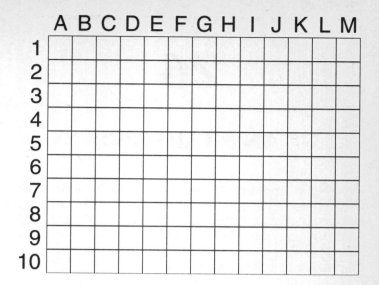

Write the answer to each clue, letter by letter, in the corresponding squares of the diagram. (As a help, about 2/3 of the letters will be used twice.) Then, by following the proper path through the completed diagram, solvers may discern a verse of some sort.

CLUES

1 Lacking strength, you and I will take a fifth of whiskey (4) (G9 K10 B10 E1)

2 He made the rules for athletic club in the midst of depression (5) (F2 M9 K3 H1 A9)

3 "String" spelled with a double-E? (5) (F9 K1 F1 J5 J9)

4 Swimwear shown by family during premiere of *Batman 2* (6) (L7 F6 C3 I10 K7 D2)

5 Big house . . . almost six feet (6) (I6 J2 L9 C10 B6 D5)

6 Land after failure of plane trip (6) (H9 L5 I10 F5 J4 J8)

7 If you quit, you never graduate — take the finals later (6) (I6 E10 B4 H5 G2 A3)

8 Maximum number after end of month (6) (M8 J3 H8 C6 C10 J8)

9 Mid-Western sorceress has a spasm (6) (L9 C9 L1 I1 A8 F4)

10 Woman, greeting knight, takes it to heart (6) (E3 L3 I1 G3 C5 J5)

11 Fraction of wet ground, 50 feet high (7) (M1 C9 A5 I9 I4 F9 M8)

12 Novices slave over chicken having a hint of mustard (8) (I4 D3 J6 K4 C7 B1 B5 E7)

13 The maniac holds back full-bosomed wife (8) (I2 E6 L4 B7 M6 B10 F3 D4)

14 Upon return, I cheer a true American spy (8, 2 wds.) (M6 B2 F3 B8 G3 K2 E5 L3)

15 In the interim, self-conflict? (8) (K5 A9 J2 H4 I7 G6 D5 A5)

16 Cords used for wrapping "Instant Junk Food" (8) (I7 G9 L1 B3 C3 H8 K10 M4)

17 Going around in circles in a West Virginia city (8) (A10 J7 F8 D8 J1 H2 G7 K9)

18 Baseball team's bat stolen by my team — very wrong (8, 2 wds.) (M10 A2 D6 E8 B5 H10 L8 L2)

19 Homes in on bad liquor (9) (B1 D10 M5 C4 K4 I8 D2 J10 A3)

20 Nothing that is right is more indecent (9) (C4 K8 M2 G8 A2 E8 D6 I3 F7)

21 Boys will eat one kind of Mexican sauce for money (9) (D9 H2 G5 M5 I9 E4 L6 H7 H10)

22 Female Indian monarch is complaining (9) (B9 E9 H5 B2 K1 E1 I5 K7 G8)

23 Starting tomorrow, poet has three months (9) (B4 D3 G6 K5 E4 G1 C8 H6 F7)

24 Thin one occupies most of residence after getting paid back (10) (L10 F1 G10 M3 C7 B8 E7 A6 E10 E2)

25 Improved state of a form of government — about time (10) (A4 I3 C6 J3 H7 J6 E5 K2 D1 G4)

26 Girl in a story rewritten in the album (10) (H3 F4 M2 G5 L7 C1 D7 F10 A7 K8)

27 Kind of run-down car in which Edison moved about (11) (A8 L6 H4 D9 F6 C2 J9 G2 K6 A1 M7)

28 Talkative drunk has large amounts left (11, hyph.) (H1 A6 M9 E2 C1 L4 F10 B7 M3 D8 L10)

26

ANY TAKERS?

The eight unclued Across entries form a familiar sequence.

ACROSS

8 Eager to follow leader of majestic Biblical land (5)

12 In schoolbag, a vegetable plant (5)

14 Gold taken from country band (5)

15 Bachelor currently runs big game (5)

16 Lacing it with a hint of rum will make beer more substantial (6)

17 Paintings of Middle Earth (3)

18 Suit is torn because of weak piece of nylon thread (8)

20 Liberal monarchs losing initial faith (7)

23 Some Europeans like a bridge? (7)

26 Man enters having the power to walk (5)

29 Nosy person not nearly suppressed by bribe (5)

31 In favor of pardon, oddly (3)

32 Woman with a pair of foreign articles (4)

33 Mondrian abstract originally a religious painting (5)

34 Boy finishing off a snake (3)

35 About to interrupt the cardinal (5)

36 Play with grease and matches (6)

37 Female to perform lead in *Equus* (3)

38 What goes round and round and is dyed blue? (4)

DOWN

1 Chief is calling from the Center of Finances (6)

2 People study a collection of works about sovereign's heart operation (12)

3 Skate around surface of rink? It's a funny thing (6)

4 Carrier has 1,000 animal crackers (7)

5 Departure time is moved up? Wow! (4)

6 NRA dropping lead shot — it's found in hoppers (7)

7 Badly . . . even half badly (6)

8 Table acquired by James Arness (4)

9 Regard being made over as a piece of cake? (11)

10 Olympics' top female gets perfect scores frequently (6)

11 $1,000 added to handle the equipment (4)

13 A contemptible sort, woman or man (4)

18 Frightened at the outset, lady moved slightly and recoiled (8)

19 English horse corralled by Peg Young (7)

21 Got some shuteye and made a pile? (6)

22 Let's see pitcher anger arbiter (6)

24 A girl's skirts are glistening (6)

25 Train is located south of popular place to stay (5)

27 Tenors dividing $50.00 in gambling game (5)

28 Prevent pet eating piece of broccoli (5)

29 Full-time employee at termination, outwardly unhappy (5)

30 Crew flies high without pilot? (4)

27
THE LAST SHALL BE FIRST

Across clues are out of sequence, with enumerations withheld. To help you place their answers, note that the last letter of each one is the first letter of the next, in order through the diagram. (Also, the last letter of the last is the first letter of the first.)

ACROSS

a Reason to record on a computer chip

b Call for one who lifts a barber's device

c Epic tale of woe, in error, written Hebraically?

d Dressed in opposite sex's clothes, take top prize in raffle

e Part of leg twisted . . . Spanish hero has limp

f Little by little, praise a football lineman's opposition?

g Feeling a bit of pain inside, overcome by rum drink

h Trouble translating Rupert Brooke's earliest

i Operatic hero ran, a bit shy with the ladies

j Have dinner disrupted by "Wild Man" L. Tanner?

k Act of pressing suit and shirt, torn during government overthrow

l Is one caught in trenches, running back from Jurassic beast?

m *Time* article penned by poor journalist in ready-made clothing (hyph.)

n Broken up by company's setback, family moves

DOWN

1 Left hog fat outside (8)

2 They impersonate police officers around the end of January 1st (8)

3 Hotels in north and south (4)

4 Harder to find entrance to room in rear building (5)

5 Woman that is most ample? (6)

6 Original murderer turned up in B-3 (6)

7 Cardinal voting in favor at hearing (4)

8 Portion of church to cave in . . . the rear half only (4)

9 Over 500 years? Zounds! (4)

10 Refuse to accept I'd turned sickly-looking (8)

11 Tell a lady to be casual (8)

12 Stirring soup is work (4)

13 Type of military attack could be faster (6)

14 Turkish commander and holy man may be shocked (6)

15 As we are not bound to take an oath (5)

16 Project requires excellent burlap fiber (4)

28

SQUARE WHEELS

The first letter of each clue answer goes in the corresponding space, with the rest of the letters proceeding clockwise or counterclockwise to trace the perimeter of a square. The first letters are not necessarily in the corners of squares.

CLUES

1 Asserts worker is showing the back of the hand (8)

2 Read top of soda container (4)

3 The US is involved in grand-scale legislation excluding some New Englanders (16)

4 Wear a G-string . . . veils . . . old clothes (4)

5 Crossing meadows, I located a storage structure (4)

6 Finished writing some proverbs (4)

7 Murder case experts (4)

8 Oakland ballplayer caught by New York ballplayer from the east side (4)

9 Press agent, somewhat wise (4)

10 Leg bruise, ultimately from competition (4)

11 Headed back around large valley (4)

12 Berlin's song told a story (4)

13 Club team's leader among one old king's attendants (8)

14 Foreign anthem makes man revolt, broken up by return of WW2 victors (12)

15 Make 50-50 figure (4)

16 English free verse written during spring shows doggedness (12)

17 Writing of former partner in *Times* (4)

18 After the introduction, science is dull (4)

19 Number on fastener held by twisted screw, i.e., reading this way (16)

20 Native American woman trapped in snow and ice at the end (8)

21 Awkward college sophomore's last to enter forest in New York (8)

22 Animal tamer started wearing a slicker (8)

23 In Paris, I will accept grant given in jest (4)

24 Goes off, taking eastern railroads (4)

25 Front end has a feather (4)

26 Let's split (4)

27 Child, back in kindergarten, left a region of Canada (8)

28 Nick Nolte's nose caught by jab (4)

29 Big number is cut . . . vandal disrupting cast needn't cut in (16, 2 wds.)

30 In part, counterordered, nullified, or revoked! (8)

31 A&E features the essence of Leontyne Price (4)

32 In Spain, young male knight in love (4)

33 Kansas City Royal accepts no criticism (8)

34 Tennis star suppressed by more athletic person's unable to answer? (12)

35 Corpse in wrong plot (8)

36 Eco novel about leader of political cartel (4)

37 Dashing hunk is former baseball commissioner (4)

38 Shakes containers (4)

39 Malone, smuggling art, wounded fatally (8)

40 Call the old ladies (4)

41 *The Nation* includes article on true love of the stage (12)

42 Frat man uncovered a foul odor (4)

43 Measure Mr. Young's parrots (4)

44 Scoundrel called for remedy (4)

45 Tax bureau confiscates $1,000 and causes anger (4)

29

CALL 1-900-PUZZLES

Each answer is to be entered as a sequence of digits, not letters, following the standard layout of a telephone keypad. (Thus, A, B, or C = 2; D, E, or F = 3; etc.) But be careful: In all likelihood, a digit will not represent the same letter Across as it does Down. So, if the answer to 1 Across begins with, say, M, then the answer to 1 Down could begin with either M, N, or O.

ACROSS

1 Beam when reading some of Margaret Farrar's rejection letters? (6)

7 A boss rebuffed about fifty old people? (6)

12 At first, bring a gadget in the tub (7)

13 Gentiles leave club, and I'm following (5)

14 Without a hint of mercy, club an animal (6)

15 Polar phenomena reviewed as a topic in Astronomy 101 (7)

16 Part of the arm is somewhat painful, naturally (4)

17 Lively dance shown by one amid mawkishness (5)

18 Bedcover in *Good Housekeeping* owned by an admirer (6)

20 Fabulous flyer, near speed of light, going through low country (7)

23 Start to engrave "C" in black circle on car's rear bumper? (7)

27 Southern extremist group captures Paris' lead model (6)

30 Drunk decks sailor with wooden shoe (5)

31 Get out of the way of a bird (4)

32 Vessel gets through blind (7, hyph.)

34 Wrangler is reluctant to take broken bow (6)

35 Power could (5)

36 Dry plastic wrap preserving a piece of ham (7)

37 Persian king and queen involved in double-crosses? (6)

38 Being absent rocks workplace (6)

DOWN

1 Thin lady with peripheral vision (6)

2 S&L engages expert investigator on TV (7)

3 Waste time with daughter in valley (6)

4 Gave crackers for big star (4)

5 Some 500 to rise before holy man and ruler (6)

6 Hairdresser, any day now, will take a ship (7)

8 Summon First Lady to accept fine (5)

9 *Can-Can* good for colorization? (7)

10 Overwhelmed by K2, I'm surprised I joined military outfit? (5)

11 Funny show is rerun — pilot of *Three's Company* at noon (6)

19 Ball turned up in path of beast (7)

21 Vegetable with most of pie filling, say (7)

22 Lacks the wherewithal, in a bar (7)

23 Dull . . . even without the audience's intrusion? (6)

24 Perverse chap has managed to find a type of rock (6)

25 Making fun of Peg during drunken spree (6)

26 Love in Spain . . . you might be bounced (6)

28 Head of the United Nations prepares to take off (5)

29 Go up to get new hair color (5)

33 Number 4 encased in iron (4)

30

MY HOME, SWEET HOME

In this acrostic, black squares are not given, but spaces will eventually appear between words.

CLUES

A Without question, leave in defeat (8) (B11 K6 M1 K13 O11 B8 B4 I7)

B After live comeback, crooner is in decline (6) (A4 E12 F8 A2 D6 O4)

C Little woman and I come in to provide answer (9) (D1 P11 P10 A3 H13 D3 B7 C6 O8)

D Mash a vegetable (6) (H5 N11 A11 C9 H7 N3)

E Hard water flowing down (9) (B6 B1 E13 L8 F7 A8 D4 N2 J9)

F On the contrary — an excellent gas (6) (F1 F12 H2 G6 G10 I4)

G Call operator and express a desire for a little gold? (9) (H3 J11 A5 C7 H1 D10 P9 J8 I2)

H Subsequently, have faith in candor (9) (N7 L5 F13 N9 O3 P1 I5 K11 L9)

I One of the twins, an intruder in the garden, started wearing shirt (10) (C8 K5 G11 N8 B2 L4 O12 I11 P6 H9)

J Serious attempt in favor of thwarting Newt (6) (A13 M6 B3 I3 G4 M5)

K Show of dissent from crowd in front of police precinct house (12) (O1 N6 L10 M3 C11 E6 O2 H8 B12 G9 D13 J4)

L Extremely outspoken Ethiopian leader's first name? (6) (M8 C1 P5 D8 O9 M4)

M Joint returns are shaky if one billion isn't accounted for (5) (C2 K9 C13 P4 N12)

N Scarf from someone who's amorous with principal (11) (M11 O7 D5 B10 N13 G1 K10 J12 O6 F10 F4)

O Southern singer/actress bathes northern hockey star with sponge? (9) (C12 H10 N5 D11 I1 F9 P3 G8 G5)

P Due to have indefinite number in possession (5) (M2 F3 I8 I10 I6)

Q NPR featuring broadcasting from Italy, but not for money (9) (I13 E5 A7 L2 P12 E2 E9 H4 I12)

R Tight end finally understanding about rush (7) (K4 A6 M7 A12 J1 M13 I9)

S Before pilot eats seafood, Hugo doesn't have to leave in a snit (9) (E10 L13 B5 A1 E11 A9 K7 K1 L12)

T You feel terrible when there's no love in view (6) (E3 D7 P8 F2 F5 F11)

U I approach home seriously (9, 2 wds.) (L11 H6 N10 G7 J3 A10 J2 P13 G12)

V Mimic has cash — about $1,000 (6) (M10 L7 O13 K3 K12 L1)

A B C D E F G H I J K L M N O P

1
2
3
4
5
6
7
8
9
10
11
12
13

31 ADDITIONAL

Answers to Clues 1-12 are 6-letter words, each to be written in the corresponding space. Answer to Clues a-1 are 7-letter words, each formed by adding a letter to one of the 6-letter words and then rearranging; write each of these answers in the space to the right of the appropriate 6-letter word. Answers to Clues m-x are 8-letter words, similarly derived from the 7-letter words; place them accordingly. In alternate rows, write the first added letter in the box at the right and the second added letter in the box at the right; in the other rows, do the opposite.

1			
2			
3			
4			
5			
6			
7			
8			
9			
10			
11			
12			

SIXES

1 Latin : French :: English : Irish
2 Wearing cravat, undone, and a piece of jewelry
3 Point of a compass cuts through short line in geometry
4 Rodent finally running free in Spanish retreats
5 Heart of ozone layer destroyed . . . she had a cow
6 Send back fellow in debt, symbolically
7 Concerning a boy's logic
8 Conductor turned crimson on "A" train
9 Seal gets in convertible
10 A hint of mystic incense in trough
11 Doll, nude, has pair of biggies?
12 Brown rice (defrosted?) my group prepared

SEVENS

a US native is correct about Rhode Island
b Borne by donkey, Penny moves upward
c Charms rebellious oarsmen
d Using more words, in general . . . that is padding (abbr.)
e 1,000-pounder(?) is in it for noted collaborator
f Bit of gin finer, in a way, with lots of ice
g Don't start to excavate saltpeter — it'll burn

h Nobleman virtually assumes Ivy League school to be more trustworthy
i Cheating, as regards friend overseas — no good
j Woman in a rush is delighted
k The USSR demolished bars once more
l Arrangement of chairs is foremost for sumptuous dining

EIGHTS

m Symbolic story would be utterly sensational if error were deleted
n Live with alumnus in the French capital
o Chap in center of garbage barge
p Stick around — audience is disappearing
q Big caber tossed in game
r East Indian princess covered in something sticky and bright red
s Revolutionary soldier enters into real crafty plot
t I dream in *High Noon*
u Northern sect was involved with televised information
v Scandinavian calls Mr. Reagan "misguided"
w More lively South African port
x Finished with women and birds

32
FROM TOP TO BOTTOM

One answer in each row across (except for the *top* and *bottom*) is unclued. These answers, read in order from *top* to *bottom*, form a chain, each item somehow related to the next.

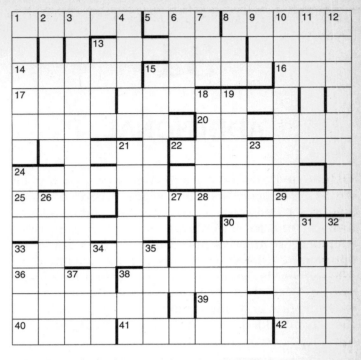

ACROSS

1 Took notice of area among crawfishing places (5, 2 wds.)
5 One foot to the rear (3)
8 Opera singers making a comeback — some miss a beat (5)
13 Surroundings in which I am buried in mud, most of the way (6)
14 I will infiltrate lower-class revolutionary association (5)
16 One-time worker (3)
17 Distance followed by our sulky (5)
20 Sale item: grated nuts (6, 2 wds.)
22 Falsely claim he is an archangel (7)
24 Benefit to take place, followed by dance (6)
25 No dessert for artist (4)
30 Woman receives help from servants (5)
33 Major-General Olson ignoring boy's perverse hangup (6)
36 Circumference of Aral Sea region (4)
39 Delays in booths (6)
40 Dr. Strangelove at last accepts a challenge (4)
41 We're mistakenly taking a couple of shirts from drier? No (6)
42 Survey everything, essentially! (3)

DOWN

1 Small mix of water and dirt, for example, seen in the mirror?! (6)
2 A sound imitating bugs (6)
3 Article describes one in the rear being victorious (10)
4 Nina's sister Peg gets turned on (5)
6 Movie retrospective of married life ends abruptly (4)
7 Afternoon reception group robbed of 1,000 (3)
8 Coach is initially behind my crew (3)
9 It's like beginning to smoke dope (3)
10 Austere painting with 9" border (7)
11 Rich treat seen by Butch's pal outside of North Carolina (6)
12 Engineer toiling to frame a carving (8)
13 Expression of lament in early hours (4)
15 American township bordered by gulf that's whirling and windy (7)
18 Brownie coated with cheese (4)
19 In Caesar's terms, fifty behold Italian town (5)
21 Navy invades Dalmatian group near a region of Asia Minor (5)
23 Hourly rerunning of *Harry O* (6)
24 Jazz hit (3)
26 Midwestern city I described in comic opera (6)
27 Nonconformist female . . . one in a haze? (6)
28 Man protected by Prime Directive (6)
29 Drink very quietly, wearing high silk hat (6)
30 Dull spouse embracing Ford model (5)
31 Mat in front of door, slippery (5)
32 E.g., taste most of breath freshener (5)
33 Movie star's son and daughter (4)
34 Make fun of judge — do an impersonation (4)
35 Horse manure on the borders (4)
37 Audience in the arena (3)
38 Do some housework! (3)

33

AROUND THE BEND

Each answer is to be entered *diagonally* in the grid, with its first and last letters (though not necessary respectively) in the correspondingly numbered squares, and the path of the answer turning exactly once to form an L. The letters in the central 18 squares will spell an appropriate phrase.

1	2		3	4	5			6	7	8	9
10		11			12	13		14			15
16		17			18	19					
20	21	22	23		24				25	26	
					27	28	29		30		
		31	32			33		34	35		36
37		38	39		40		41	42		43	
		44					45	46			
47	48	49		50		51	52	53	54		
55				56				57		58	59
60				61	62		63				
64		65		66				67		68	
69	70	71	72	73	74	75	76		77	78	79

CLUES

1-19 Chair occupied by unknown Oregon legislator (7)

2-31 Woman's name given by football player wearing lingerie (6)

3-27 Odd number that wouldn't be if reduced by 1/3 of six? (5)

3-31 Smuggling diamonds, British crew gets on (6)

4-25 Discouraged woman trapped in old man's body? (6)

5-44 Famous nurse had to be injected with cocaine, ultimately (8)

5-57 Before turning haggard, throw up (10)

6-15 Wild animal slaughtered fowl (4)

6-35 Loud cry from lady with underclothing? (6)

7-26 Former talk-show host not running in traffic? (4)

7-30 Create small puppet (5)

8-36 Persuaded to pen poem without spirit (6)

9-34 Strong, intelligent woman replaces me (6)

10-11 Mother desired a model's features (3)

10-20 A room or a wing (3)

12-17 Notice I tacked at the front entrance (4)

13-26 Prance about, for one (5)

14-29 Spider, full of energy, turning the tide (4)

14-46 Basketball team accepts $1,000 to become football team (7)

16-24 Courteous author gets drunk (6)

16-37 Blackguard to swindle chief of police (5)

18-48 Raven flying around live plant (7)

19-51 Woman lived in speakeasy (7)

21-38 Mineral obtained from chemical (4)

21-60 Type of shark meat near stove (8, hyph.)

22-34 Chicago businessman's evasive speaking (7)

23-25 Facts about old car company's principles (7)

25-68 Changed trains to D.C.? Never (9)

28-63 Touching a male sunbather? (7)

32-73 Economist, wrongly informed about center of trade, loses nothing (8)

33-55 Beyond South American river, eat fish (7)

34-76 Moving around, crossing through frontier (8)

35-66 Display of derring-do is source of vexation in traveling abroad (7)

36-59 Master builder essentially has merit (5)

38-42 Disney employee's profit included in cost (7)

39-46 Maroon fiber (6)

39-72 Comedian assumes it's perversely violent (7)

40-54 Silly group turns right, heading east (5)

41-72 Bouncy piece of music — it's a lengthy recessional (7)

43-75 Lodger, holding a white key, to come back in (7)

45-78 Fuel rating = 1/100 . . . half-tank (6)

46-77 He wins, but angrily complains (6)

47-50 Religious belief is harbored by Democrat (5)

49-71 Words from latter half of Pinter manuscript (5)

52-74 You may comprehend singer's closing number (5)

53-71 Salespeople . . . almost all back after five (7)

56-64 Fights with father, crossing streets (5)

58-79 Avoid a big star taking heroin (4)

59-78 Cat's head is stuck in toilet — that's crazy (4)

60-75 Fan eating piece of sliced chicken (7)

61-77 Missile of war, or explosive (5)

62-67 Cape worn by English student (4)

64-74 Southern gallery features Utrillo's greatest work of art (6)

65-69 "Myself to follow, myself to follow" — opening from Robert Frost (4)

70-76 A little creature . . . perhaps it's a bee (7)

34

FITTING

Some answers are not fit to be in the diagram; the way to remedy this lack of fitness is to obey the instructions at 1 Across.

ACROSS

1 *See instructions* (12, 3 wds.)
11 Chop large eagle's tail feathers (6)
13 Region in Far East (4)
14 Number three, perhaps (5)
15 Alabama baseball team in compound (7)
16 Earlier article in favor of unlimited sex (5)
19 For the second time, test trailer hitches (7)
20 Crosses sticks to conceal hole (5)
22 Burglar originally caught by watchful prince (6)
23 Kit returns love letters left in auto trunk (7)
24 Russian distance runner finally passes athlete in lead, Polish (7)
26 Initially, guard your pawn with rook (3)
29 Pete Rose is tired (7)
32 Western bad guy to block lines of carts (12)
36 John Lennon's biggest discs (3)
37 Announcer's work on soundtracks will grow by 100% (6)
39 Top-rated mid-afternoon broadcast (3)
40 Intimidate 1/3 of coworkers (3)
41 Birds' hit-and-run is central to Astros' initial defeats (11)
43 Clamor after love god (4)
44 Confusion shown by band in endless pursuit (5)
46 Check some vegetables (3)
48 Hispanic actor in experimental lab in western state, a bit shy (9)
50 Storybook villain's smile initially captures hearts (6)
51 Crossing from another country (4)
52 Pale man, inwardly bashful (4)
53 Thin, crisp slices of food put back in medium oven (10, 2 wds.)

DOWN

2 Doughnut near cereal (3)
3 Old Latin book carried by awfully choosy student (9)
4 Increase accepted by housekeepers (3)
5 I'll be darned! Ultimately, eating right is rude (7, hyph.)
6 Member of a team carrying ball, scrambling to spike, breaks through (10)
7 Talks endlessly of values (6)
8 Some nervous people bristle in a bombing (10, hyph.)
9 Recipient finished taking high tea (7)
10 Prodigals will receive outrageous bill from fascinating people (12)
11 Middle Earth, perhaps (5)
12 Listening device hidden in the Armory (3)
17 He jumps back, supported by gravity; . . . (4)
18 . . . he jumps back from chamber (3)
21 There's a player full of energy (3)
25 It'll make holes in everything, reportedly (3)
27 Bucking trend, pay attention to details (8)
28 Explorer initially bags a large snake (6)
30 Where drivers pay extra to circumvent lines on median of highway (9)
31 Mae West harbors sheep (4)
33 Gangsters eating LifeSavers? Curses (7)
34 Train due after bus drops us off, being pokey? (8)
35 Sausages, like cooked fish, vitamin-enriched (9)
38 Dodger pitcher, in Brewers' cap, ran around (6)
39 Ask the man, three feet short, with breathing problem (6)
40 Place to pause with man in deep sleep (5)
42 Scottish baron nested articles (5)
45 Get lost in SoHo when hospital is relocated (4)
47 Hit number . . . just about (4)
49 Try for a hit with "Am I Blue?" (3)

35
ACROSTIC

In this acrostic, spaces between words are left for the solver to determine.

CLUES

A Big story about Nils Washington, a lumberjack (11) (89 109 163 38 123 71 126 94 177 18 45)

B Quality of one princess in spotless condition? (14) (169 51 84 97 187 135 15 122 69 181 105 26 59 4)

C Boys left spots (4) (162 133 47 176)

D Blessing in diary written by girl in mirror (12, 2 wds.) (78 32 108 11 183 67 170 64 131 37 155 93)

E I'm one to be inhibited by my resistance (8) (137 167 1 185 114 72 152 196)

F Pair of articles on McEntire's debut in country music? (6) (119 27 75 156 39 139)

G On horseback, medical officer sought Cockney? (7) (25 164 48 3 22 95 92)

H Chief of staff and ex-Defense Secretary catching opening of *Cabin Boy* in New York city (11) (129 96 21 141 151 116 49 13 190 28 88)

I Drove to terminal in Milwaukee, in German car I abandoned (6) (194 144 121 154 61 74)

J Some members of sextet, on too frequently, going over explanation (8) (160 5 58 173 43 184 107 148)

K Soldier goes back to nearly free housing up north (6) (79 182 127 110 171 145)

L Diet soda — one consumed by runner, with a vegetable (8) (34 102 81 166 191 98 52 150)

M Complicates problem, being somewhat ghostly (11) (168 20 44 82 125 193 2 100 56 175 120)

N Wrinkle . . . or hairline? (6) (161 68 17 195 90 149)

O Good man, braced by your help, made new seat covers and such (10) (192 117 23 46 9 80 172 36 91 130)

P Low comedy introduced by female freeloader (7) (65 188 14 142 174 55 35)

Q Screws up Schubert medley (8) (62 7 112 189 76 146 40 138)

R Timeless wit, embraced by the French! (5) (99 70 158 86 41)

S Police force in eastern Alaska to get environmentalist (8) (12 136 157 83 178 66 143 165)

T I walk when caught by pitch — in retrospect, it may take a little hop (6) (118 104 140 101 63 53)

U Awkward marshals win duel with club (8) (33 73 115 42 124 87 180 128)

V Lady provided dandy rise (7) (132 50 31 19 179 6 111)

W Counter man, ingesting "pink lady," is set (9) (113 186 16 85 134 106 10 29 54)

X Small-time tenor, in fact, shows a desire for kisses? (10, 2 wds.) (8 147 77 24 153 57 159 30 103 60)

1E	2M	3G	4B	5J	6V	7Q	8X	9O	10W	11D	12S	13H	14P	15B	16W	17N	18A	19V	20M	21H	22G
23O	24X	25G	26B	27F	28H	29W	30X	31V	32D	33U	34L	35P	36O	37D	38A	39F	40Q	41R	42U	43J	44M
45A	46O	47C	48G	49H	50V	51B	52L	53T	54W	55P	56M	57X	58J	59B	60X	61I	62Q	63T	64D	65P	66S
67D	68N	69B	70R	71A	72E	73U	74I	75F	76Q	77X	78D	79K	80O	81L	82M	83S	84B	85W	86R	87U	88H
89A	90N	91O	92G	93D	94A	95G	96H	97B	98L	99R	100M	101T	102L	103X	104T	105B	106W	107J	108D	109A	110K
111V	112Q	113W	114E	115U	116H	117O	118T	119F	120M	121I	122B	123A	124U	125M	126A	127K	128U	129H	130O	131D	132V
133C	134W	135B	136S	137E	138Q	139F	140T	141H	142P	143S	144I	145K	146Q	147X	148J	149N	150L	151H	152E	153X	154I
155D	156F	157S	158R	159X	160J	161N	162C	163A	164G	165S	166L	167E	168M	169B	170D	171K	172O	173J	174P	175M	176C
177A	178S	179V	180U	181B	182K	183D	184J	185E	186W	187B	188P	189Q	190H	191L	192O	193M	194I	195N	196E		

36

7, 8, 9

Clues are listed in alphabetical order by their answer lengths.

SEVENS

1 An award for Broadway musical's lead? Just the opposite
2 A signet securing voter's mark on second of rulings, bypassing Congress?
3 Oakland ballplayer . . . extremely timid, extremely pale
4 Ultimate bit of praise to boost the man — my kind word
5 Make weary by crossing the USA in a hurry
6 Eric and his son returned a flycatcher?
7 Speaks, after finally changing channels
8 Flight attendant puts in very high mirrors
9 I would describe *Ain't Misbehavin'* "excellent afternoon performance"
10 Sees tyros embracing the wrong TV character?
11 Hole in orange tree seen from behind rocks
12 Dad's eating a pickle, in sleepwear
13 Lead everybody around in game
14 Alter the photo? About time — I'm in pain
15 Go around with beau, back to evacuated village
16 Concluding parts? Name one, name one

EIGHTS

17 Conservative tailor has simple wool
18 Building frozen shut at the entrance? I have key
19 Inscriptions in stove-pipe hats
20 Exceedingly round "O" put into words?

NINES

21 Through wearing infants' casual wear
22 $100 contribution, making a deposit in the che
23 Dunce, lost in a whirl, sought advice
24 Randy Quaid has flower and cocktails
25 Ready-made to accommodate audience
26 Something that smells in tabloid in foreign country
27 One of the teeth has one cavity . . . initially, it'
all the same
28 Most sprightly relative I involved in joke
29 Explorer, time and time again, dwelling in large tent
30 Composer Mr. Porter has to watch
31 An informer runs, intercepting information of chutists
32 One caught in rain carried a tip
33 Puts off punishing one breaking into game preserve
34 Ship full of men caught in rising current — they'll sink to the bottom
35 Fabric in V-neck originally worn by the Spanish ex-soldier
36 Talkative quality of left-leaning senator and one page caught in fix?

37

PINWHEEL

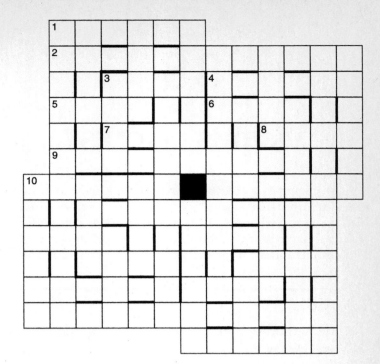

The diagram has four-way symmetry; i.e., if you rotate it 90, 180, or 270 degrees it will look the same. Clues have been divided into sets of four, with one answer belonging in the numbered Across space and the others belonging in the three symmetrically equivalent spaces.

CLUES

1 "Pink Parrots" for a group of singers (6)
Quick snooze taken by agent (6)
Western event sent us reeling (6)
Pilot, for example, back in 1927, for example (6)

2 Man's course, I'm sorry to say (?), includes traveling north (12)
Go ask about Leonard Wilder's music show (12, 3 wds.)
With everyone else inside, boy to count backwards for one on the mat? (12, 2 wds.)
California city worker joins a pair of bands in South America (12, 2 wds.)

3 Challenge excellent club (4)
"Crossing stage" — a stage direction (4)
Rod rejects advice (4)
Chaste woman conceals worry (4)

4 Boarding vessel, live in secret (6)
Snake bites general while dozing (6)
Eve shuffled in with our work (6)
Destroyed in Round One (6)

5 Raspberry sliced by large knife (4)
Hauls garbage, primarily through Latin America (4)
To spot an amphibian (4)
It's used for carrying sculptures back at end of day (4)

6 Matron angry about error (4)
Catcall gives man escalating distress (4)

Stepped down a bit, from the other side (4)
Neurosurgeon possesses drive (4)

7 A sailor's final leave from ship (4)
Your author, before an alien encounter (4)
Bug seen in milk shake's container (4)
Bird-hare hybrid? (4)

8 Greek character gets beat up halfway? (4)
Final notice — no information in the computer (4)
Show-biz union claims comedian ultimately made music (4)
Man occupying South Dakota shack (4)

9 Men at the Tower losing face in defeat — drinks all around (10)
FBI head, senior estate owner (10)
In Pennsylvania theater, Pee-Wee nearly having a fit (10)
Limitless rum consumed by politician, one involved in rendezvous with chicken farmer (10)

10 Bachelor comes into money in a section of Algiers (6)
Bird of prey disguised as parrot (6)
Leader of Yokohama goes in to sound the horn on a Japanese car (6)
Unknown magic word almost held up holidays (6)

38

VICIOUS CIRCLES

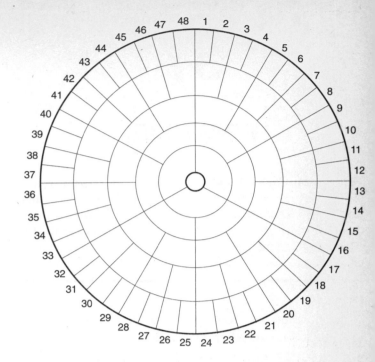

Each answer is a 6-letter word. The letters are to be entered from the circumference to the center, but always in mixed order. When the diagram is complete, the outer circle will contain an appropriate 8-word quotation, followed by the name of its most famous speaker.

CLUES

1 Pitched advertisement printed with green and red border

2 Diamond ring put back in prized tree

3 Anger a sportscaster

4 Den mother had finally left, confounded

5 Standard promotion before end of June or March

6 Doctor, mimic, and dry-goods dealer

7 In bottomless pot, concocted ointment

8 Man wearing cloak, at rear of field, put up tents

9 Refuge found in hideaway, in shadow

10 Where flowers grow in grand forest

11 Gave a speech . . . expect this to cause spat?

12 Getting a just-passing mark, fail to be enthusiastic

13 Kind old actor

14 A second-rate street in Europe

15 Forbidden poet's voice

16 Up north, an egg sandwich?

17 Conservative living in fear? That's unusual

18 Plunderer races madly to capture king

19 Places to battle one returning with more marbles?

20 One who catches TBS' latest broadcast the second time around

21 Ex-president to leave, heading west to circle globe

22 Bone of contention? One is overcome by it

23 Birds run through sticks

24 Holy parcel of land in South Dakota

25 Cook carries red flower?

26 Masher violated women's groups

27 One who intends to be more contemptible?

28 Opera for Andretti, Unser, et al?

29 Unfortunately, dressing room has warning signals

30 Smells a rat, obviously maintaining a suspicion initially

31 Cry about being involved in swindle

32 Evasively ask me about foremost of radio manufacturers

33 Salt on cuckoo's claws

34 Boy has a look in pub

35 Unnamed writer breaking hundreds of rules

36 Where you can bet it's "C," as in "circle"

37 Alternatively, catch leftist newspapers

38 One of the Stones cheers, making a comeback in performance

39 Trunk almost filled with sailor's drums

40 Take in some cabs or buses

41 French composer disrupted by rare parody

42 After the debut, TV interviewer makes changes

43 Found the French royal home

44 Criticize the man after jazz rendition

45 Fancy headgear shown by Astaire, dancing incessantly

46 Backs around labyrinth's center paths

47 In paintings, see small southeastern state

48 Reportedly, they satisfy lecherous men

39

SEE THE USA

Letters around the border of the completed diagram will reveal a round-trip tour of eight US cities, the last letter of each being the first letter of the next. Unchecked letters in this tour may be arranged to spell RE: AWAY IN U.S. VAN.

ACROSS

9 Catty remark from one hampered by $1,000 debt (5)
10 Hint: Momentarily maintaining high C (7)
12 Upon return, Georgia tenants rub me the wrong way, causing resentment (7)
14 Desires to be with independent women (6)
15 Live outside east end of city for so long (3)
16 Lacking humor inhibits you (7)
17 Takes part in Gainsborough retrospective (4)
19 Laotian refusing seconds of beef (4)
20 Car essentially moves on wheels, going about 55 (4)
21 In poem, a dreamer is about to stop short (4)
23 Tease soldier with smutty matter? (5)
24 Rent tuxedo, resewn at the hems (4)
25 Little birds move wings (8)
27 Host marches to music . . . literally (5)
29 Wooden cigar boxes finally arrived (6)
31 Engineer originally engaged in combat for sport (4)
32 Piece of statuary removed from the top of one fireplace (5)
35 Bizarre idea involves gents with true madness (8)
36 Horse keeps running, running . . . it must be in shape (7)
38 Disturb cook after the entrée (4)
40 It can be remodeled into furniture (7)
41 Thief in front of crumbling castle (5)
42 In pain from small rock (4)
43 Initially, randy old man and naive cutie engaged in love affair (7)

DOWN

1 Transitional place for branch office's leader (5)
2 Young one to howl, consuming fifth of bourbon (4)
3 Cringe when former Veep calls (5)
4 Butcher's second bad cut of meat is not pulverized (8)
5 Due to support of leader of road crew (6)
6 Stop short of Ecuador's capital (4)
7 13 to push vigorously (6)
8 Methods of finding grated chocolate particles (13)
10 Singer's work? We sing when leaders trade places (6)
11 Eve is confused with our work (6)
13 7's nebulous luster (6)
18 One who employs a stud (4)
20 Somebody watching contest with hesitation (6)
22 Native from Malay island dropping a couple off (4)
26 Indication Tommy's wild about Penny (7)
28 Candelabra gives me no cheer (7)
30 Enrage radical types (6)
33 Knot made in gun barrel, oddly (5)
34 Before *The Third Man*, find Lime's first name (5)
35 Standing in entrance is unknown philanthropist (5)
37 Musical band's engagement, first in 1996? (4)
39 Cracked part of ceiling in bathroom (4)
40 Leader of choir loves to murmur (3)

40

EVERYBODY INTO THE POOL

Acrosses are to be entered normally, but one letter has been "scratched" from the wordplay in each clue; this letter is to be written on the corresponding dash below. Down clues are normal, but each answer must undergo a "break"; i.e., its letters must be entered in scrambled order. Letters on the dashes will spell a relevant phrase, as will the two unclued Down entries. Unchecked letters in the diagram may be arranged to spell SOS — I CAN BEAT GAME.

ACROSS

1 Be quiet, mixing beer and ice (7)
7 Shack is home to Puerto Rican astronaut (7)
13 Sweet treat for newswoman Roberts (6)
14 German family in a pickle (7)
16 Small can (4)
18 Beat Tom senseless, holding end of whip (5)
19 Queen's mate pursuing endless hum . . . it's an activity for some bees (7)
20 Acute knowledge (4)
21 Residing in Long Island, in general (6)
22 Poe novel about misfortune? Just the opposite — it's a lot of fun (7)
23 Chief is broken up by a bit of gross slander (6)
24 It is seen in mirror . . . wife watches (6)
25 Continues having kinky sex — nearly a dozen involved (7)
26 Walk into church yard . . . like Friar Tuck (6)
27 Misplace ring with small emerald at the top (4)
28 I love stuffing Spanish appetizer with a sort of pudding (7)
29 *Good Housekeeping*'s true spirit (5)
30 Nuisance incessantly mimics (4)
31 Cry about a dishonest person (7)
32 Not illegal, but pretty bad (6)
33 If it were not cloudy (7)
34 Look at fat follower of Wycliffe's teachings (7)

DOWN

1 A posse hurriedly suppresses fight where orators are found (9)
2 Brewery of a sort — but quickly, you'll have to think about it (9)
3 Quietly, wild geese will surround family dog (9)
4 Singing or somersaulting is stock in trade (9)
5 Voice a conjecture about a measure of space, showing a lack of clarity (9)
6 Medleys composed of hits about Hi-C mix? (9)
7 Note: it doesn't belong to argumentative friar (9)
8 Art table and globe, about $1,000, owned by strumpet (9)
9 Sculptor, a small person, almost finished *A Big Cat* (9)
10 Chopping tools given to Massachusetts basketball team (9)
11 Dealer who's shady, but noble, has sent up for it (9)
12 Nude endured distress boarding ship (9)
13 Arrived with parcel for "Arthur's Place"? (7)
15 Desire is essential to understanding cookery (7)
17 Pen serves as home to terribly lean explorer (7)

16 13 26 21 24 28 30 34 23 18 25 7 27 32 1 22 20 33 14 29 31 19

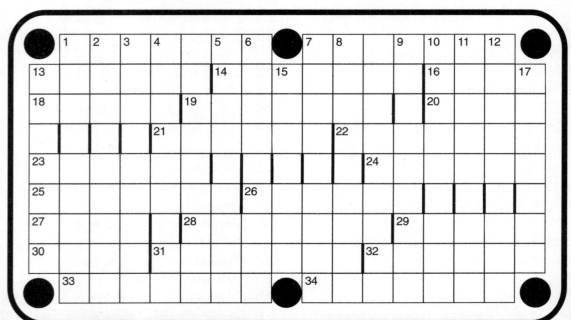

41

CARGO

Ten of the answers are too long to fit the diagram; they are to be treated in a pedestrian manner.

ACROSS

1 Spot on end of the tube (4)
4 Drink something smooth outside of Kimberley mine's entrance (8, 2 wds.)
10 Sponge, half-ripped up and full of holes (6)
12 Punch laced with corn sugar (6)
14 Ring payment (4)
15 Machine, e.g., acquired by baseball team (6)
16 Ermine ultimately fits perfectly (5)
18 Crook eats last bit of trail mix (5)
20 Lure lamb, trembling, into storm shelter? (8)
22 Business magazine found in train compartment (3)
23 Lover roared wildly (6)
24 Mr. Hefner, hosting tango dancing, to stand pat (9, 2 wds.)
25 Latitude zero entered into computer memory (4)
27 Eccentric pair somehow assumes $200 debts (10)
32 Southerner, e.g., backed up piece of information in publication (8)
33 Cereal boxes — try six (4)
34 Deserters hiding in cruiser at sea (4)
37 Incenses ump, tangling with ref at end of the Series (8)
39 Little woman found in a mine (3)
40 Extra-tiny jockeys coming in without number (9, hyph.)
43 A profile sculptured from a bright gem (8, 2 wds.)
44 Rival to show up carrying animal companion (7)
45 Monster fish (5)
46 Train due . . . and I without a partner (7)

DOWN

1 Accolades for public law examinations (8)
2 Number of letters in line deleted from standard tax form C (3)
3 Ball misplaced in pool game (4)
4 Arrest radical philosopher (6)
5 Pass her, by running beyond end of track (6)
6 "Old King's Brew" written up in restaurant rosters (8)
7 Metal drum I . . . I . . . I beat (7)
8 Nothing turned up in bottom of bag inside (6)
9 Write a couple of pieces in sharp tone — initially, it hurts (11, 3 wds.)
11 Fat lady hampered by bully (4)
12 Valley girl finally headed north (4)
13 Concealing name, confound an adventurer from Gascony (9)
17 Old royal house party in Turkey's western half (5)
19 General knowledge? Could make stomach turn a lot (8)
21 Low note from electronic musicmaker (4)
24 Time shared by us, reportedly (4)
26 Lose a large prayer book (6)
27 Blood vessels' decay thwarted by a vitamin tablet (11)
28 Without fail, a fine sex club is potentially without justification (11)
29 Amaze hiking enthusiasts (4)
30 Living in Turin, I entertained love, Italian-style? (6)
31 Quarter buried in chopped vetch (6)
35 Prince has a twisted lip (4)
36 Party-pooper conceals error (4)
38 With devious mind, priest made the previous answer? (10)
41 Start to talk about fashion (3)
42 Sumac planted in country manor (3)

42

SECTIONAL

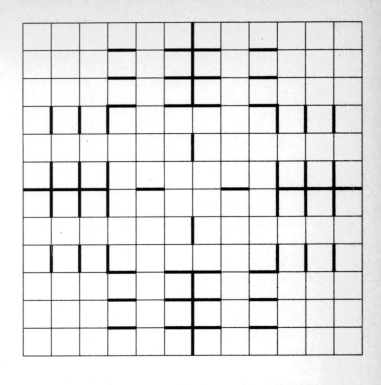

Each answer is a 6-letter word. Clues, numbered for convenience only, have been divided into sets of eight, depending on the section of the diagram in which their answers belong (one of the four corners or the center 6x6 section).

NORTHWEST

1 Antenna on TV in den picked up A&E at first
2 Renaissance begun in fashionable Italy with some pretentiousness
3 Worst musician's sound
4 Rotten bananas injected with a bit of rum
5 Ex-President sought office, keeping age disguised
6 Without much delay, grabbing a large bar
7 Father penning a true parody
8 Canvas covering for fish

NORTHEAST

9 Entertained by Maude's dancing
10 Make poor stranger tremble
11 Amorous heart is full of it, when given a boost
12 Eight punk bands love to use restraints?
13 Measure outside of round space rock
14 During 1,000th day, circles peak in Oregon (2 wds.)
15 Spies to cuss uncontrollably
16 It holds an arrangement of clover

CENTER

17 Economizes after the first and makes waves
18 Gets rid of, for example, exercising sets
19 Private Benjamin's identity conceals it
20 Guarantee to be tougher after sulphur is infused
21 Dance and make music in gay bar
22 Insults man in department store

23 Aching to receive first of invitations to English social
24 Sponsorship does not include "gold, frankincense, and myrrh"

SOUTHWEST

25 Capital stored in bank — a ransom
26 Irascible taxi driver circles right
27 Whichever total is announced, it's nine
28 Main course on salver, from what I hear
29 Messenger believed to be smuggling radium
30 Sore after gym class? Fine
31 Walk idly amid prickly shrubs
32 Initiation of young, avid American pilot

SOUTHEAST

33 A motel manager reduces
34 Catcher leaves Ty Cobb, a swinging fellow on the diamond?
35 British comic finds shelter for one, in case
36 Crash-diets before and after excellent banquets
37 Telephone stall located in square? Just the opposite
38 Sensuous lady is upset about early neutering of cats
39 Chief of police has a part in early release
40 Eddy tore wildly through 5&10

43
DOMINO THEORY

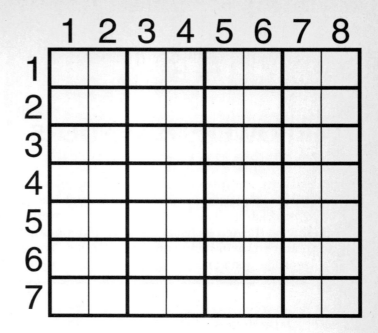

The diagram represents a standard set of double-6 dominoes, arranged in a 4x7 grid, each domino placed horizontally (as indicated by the black bars). Each domino, from double-blank to double-6, appears exactly once, the pips being represented by the letters of the clue answers. Thus, each individual square of the diagram will hold anywhere from zero to six letters, in quantities for the solver to determine. Answers to the clues for each row or column are to be entered sequentially; if a square contains two or more letters, these letters are to be used in the same order for both the row and the column.

ROWS

1 Everybody assumes Republicans run (6)
Love stories infused with slightly dramatic music your folks like? (6)
Puts restrictions on money initially offered during dice game (6)

2 Hearty pitch (3)
The old lady lost a dollar outside entrance to wildlife park (11)

3 Qualifying as father, doctor acquires twitch (13)
Rabbit fur, you say? (4)
Farmer's item that helps steer (6)

4 Leave a piece of ice in drinks for soccer players (7)
Mexican meal includes mostly fish sauce (7)
Sounds like a key part of Christmas spirit? (8)

5 Source of comfort glommed by dishonest heirs?! (6)
Who looks bad riding T-Bird? (6)
Leader of resistance, eager to imprison woman, gets carried away (8)
Figure on getting caught outside with silver ring (7)

6 Attempt to ensnare yak pulling back (9)
Drug is marijuana . . . a tiny bit (6)
Leader of Klan spotted returning to low joints? (5)
Last of the pigeons flying around a field full of moles? (9)
Poem ends ". . . in summer, with my buxom bride" (5)
Commotion, in one act (3)

7 Nice gal could be much more than just nice (7)
Chevy ultimately running stoplight back there (6)
Express sorrow — this is in from our newsroom (5)
Newspaper boss tried unsuccessfully to acquire *Globe* (6)
Servicewoman whirls, giving a bird call (3)

COLUMNS

1 Getting high? Capsule contains one fine sedative (9)
Actor's cook discovered flipping goose egg (6)
Tennis player, at eighth place in tournament, to make a switch (6)

2 Quite a few cups, empty, removed from sailing vessel (6)
The expression of gratitude in a letter (5)
Tabulation is not straight (7)
Line 1 in forged copy of insurance contract (6)

3 Bugs hidden in office at ten (mid-morning) in city building (13, 2 wds.)

4 In journal, alien is referring to food (7)
Type of macaroni stored in steel bowls (5)
Noise heard in traffic, made by horse riding back of truck (4)
Born and died in poverty (4)

5 Head of state to pack and run away (5)
I regret to say, a young woman is not fully developed (4)
Manage to make off with fifth of booze (4)
Times employees starting to strike out (5)
Stylist's original hairdo is something seedy? (5)
My group's teatime starts late (3)

6 They're used for cutting deep within — incredibly sharp points (10)
Saw Rangers' final, overwhelmed by 7-1 in last period (10)

7 Exaggerated a couple of stories and made gags? (9)
Poet's above pinching horse's ass? (6)
Smack that thing! (3)
It's held by sailor catching killer whale (4)

8 Lionel Hurt, playwright (6)
Get set up before court (5)
Run, in some pain (5)
Covering area, stranger mowed grass (6)

44
BORROWERS & LENDERS

Each Across answer loses a letter before placement in the diagram; each Down answer gains a letter (never an unchecked letter). The letter lost by the answer to the *n*th clue on the Across list is the same letter gained by the answer to the *n*th clue on the Down list. These letters, in order, spell an appropriate word.

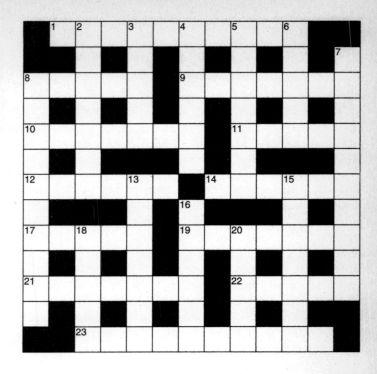

ACROSS
1 They cause delays, upsetting judge before balls (11)
8 Subways will get me back to work in the mailroom (6)
9 See wise man behind tangled vine (8)
10 Before, daughter set after old chestnuts up a tree (8)
11 Snake catches general napping (6)
12 Type of auto, wrecked Pinto, with air conditioning (7)
14 Crossing eastern part of church, 150 surrounded area (7)
17 Find colt running around one end of range (6)
19 Weak monarch in cogitation (8)
21 Catch television rerun about error made by old soldiers (8)
22 Leave Antwerp's terminal, in precious time (6)
23 Medium started in, fearing telepathic transference (11, 2 wds.)

DOWN
2 Morale shown by elf, putting energy to the fore (6)
3 Optimistic son adopted by Mr. Rogers (4)
4 Storybook child heard note from a soprano (5)
5 Coach eats a half-dozen eggs? (6)
6 Woman has hole in sandal (4)
7 Quantity of time taken by unfamiliar crew (9, 2 wds.)
8 "Oven is warm," *Voice* reprinted (9)
13 Keep me up during storm (6)
15 Embraced by woman, I'm a little beast (6)
16 Confusing question for one who takes a stand? (5)
18 Pack of sheep led by collie at first (4)
20 Letter concealed among audiotapes (4)

45

HOURGLASS

The top half of the hourglass diagram contained a quotation, but, after repeated tumblings, the grains of sand (letters) have shifted to the bottom half. Answers across are to be entered normally; answers down are to be entered with their letters scrambled (except for 13 Down, which will give the source of the quotation). The black square in the top half happens to fall between words but is otherwise insignificant.

ACROSS

4 Policeman at a nightclub (4)
10 Yearns for clothing (5)
17 Act mad about one in love with islander; . . . (8)
34 . . . "crazy love" is such a state? (8)
36 Fictional farmer, out of energy (5)
42 Sneak in before everybody else, as they say in Joisey? (5)
43 Fashion IBM's latest computer hookup (5)
47 Enthusiast traveling far to embrace English king (5)
48 They pick up shavers, reportedly (7)
51 Report of a mendicant's housing (4)
60 Lots to be got from settling book deals (9)
71 Elevator man could make it so (4)
72 Profits from returning gun (4)
88 Standard American university, with nearly everything (5)
105 In need of food outside a foreign country (7)
109 Young boy gets me busted (5)
114 Finished reading portion of Proverbs (4)
118 Left a Scout group under a burden (5)
121 Make lace and make art on the skin (6)
126 In the center of poorly lit back street (5)
128 Some violent entertainment is rather meager (6)
139 Audience's prompt to form a line (5)
144 Divided a serving of garlic (5)
146 Did Revere ride voluntarily, taking part in Revolution? (5)
162 Faxed only half of sentence (4)
166 Old man starting late, quite confused (7)
168 Street child, playing for money, loses $1,000 (5)
171 Timid moneylender, devoid of hair (3)

DOWN

2 Up front, needleworker aware of fabric (5)
13 *See instructions* (13, 2 wds.)
17 Drank, very loudly, fifth of booze in court (7)
19 Pith helmets — #1, inside and out? (5)
34 Rough street joins two New England states (6)
42 Iron taken by man or woman (6)
46 Intends to scatter seeds around can (8)
47 Big animal enthusiast left at the end of June (6)
59 A&E features *Scoundrel at My School* (7)
60 Son practically stripped reptile (5)
61 Note: I draw bust (7)
77 Checked outside, provided I gave evidence (9)
81 A little bit tense from choral work (5)
86 Ordinary selection of chef's implements (6)
89 Keep us in a spot (7)
105 Place for a frog that eats a piece of raspberry doughnut (6)
108 Sharp, as when overcome by an amount of beer (7)
112 Turn to somebody in the mirror (5)
113 Brilliant victory within seven days (5)
114 *Excitable Lady*, a number-1 book, getting a boost (9)
126 Sailor man has legal difficulty (8)
137 Units of time running into 1,000ths (6)
166 Bit of crystal gold on a light ring (6)
170 1/3 of cement is enough to fill hole, it's said (6)
171 Hockey player crossing bridge to get pouch (7)
176 Being isolated is back in style — no lie (6)
177 Army officer, in hearing, comes across as a nut (6)

TIMES BOOKS CROSSWORD ORDER FORM

VOL	ISBN	QUANTITY	PRICE	TOTAL PRICE

Random House Masterpiece Crosswords
Elegant, all-new crosswords plus profiles of famous puzzlemakers in a hardcover-spiral format.

VOL	ISBN	QUANTITY	PRICE	TOTAL PRICE
1	96373	_____	$15.00	_____

L.A. Times Sunday Crosswords
Witty, contemporary puzzles from the pages of the Los Angeles Times.

VOL	ISBN	QUANTITY	PRICE	TOTAL PRICE
5	91917-3	_____	$7.50	_____
6	91918-1	_____	$7.50	_____
7	91919-X	_____	$8.00	_____
8	91920-3	_____	$7.50	_____
9	92227-1	_____	$7.50	_____
10	92228-X	_____	$8.50	_____
11	92229-8	_____	$8.50	_____
12	92230-1	_____	$8.00	_____
13	92231-X	_____	$8.50	_____
14	92232-8	_____	$8.50	_____

Washington Post Sunday Crosswords
N.Y. Times-quality puzzles from the nation's capital.

VOL	ISBN	QUANTITY	PRICE	TOTAL PRICE
1	91933-5	_____	$8.00	_____
2	91934-3	_____	$7.50	_____
3	92109-7	_____	$8.00	_____
4	92396-0	_____	$8.00	_____

N.Y. Times Daily Crosswords
America's favorite mental exercise!

VOL	ISBN	QUANTITY	PRICE	TOTAL PRICE
30	91997-1	_____	$7.50	_____
31	92043-0	_____	$8.00	_____
32	92082-1	_____	$7.50	_____
33	92183-6	_____	$7.50	_____
34	92209-3	_____	$7.50	_____
35	92270-0	_____	$8.00	_____
36	92340-5	_____	$8.00	_____
37	92358-8	_____	$8.00	_____
38	92350-9	_____	$8.00	_____
39	92481-9	_____	$8.50	_____

N.Y. Times Sunday Crosswords
The standard by which other crosswords have been judged for more than 50 years.

VOL	ISBN	QUANTITY	PRICE	TOTAL PRICE
11	91115-6	_____	$8.00	_____
12	91166-0	_____	$8.00	_____
13	91191-1	_____	$8.00	_____
14	91681-6	_____	$8.00	_____
15	91781-2	_____	$8.00	_____
16	91839-8	_____	$8.00	_____
17	91878-9	_____	$8.00	_____
18	92268-9	_____	$8.00	_____
19	92083-X	_____	$8.00	_____
20	92451-7	_____	$8.00	_____

Very Tough Puzzles
The toughest puzzles ever published in book form!
Random House UltraHard Crosswords

VOL	ISBN	QUANTITY	PRICE	TOTAL PRICE
1	96372-5	_____	$8.00	_____
2	92482-7	_____	$8.00	_____

N.Y. Times Toughest Crosswords

VOL	ISBN	QUANTITY	PRICE	TOTAL PRICE
1	91694-8	_____	$8.00	_____
2	91828-2	_____	$9.00	_____
3	91912-2	_____	$9.00	_____
4	92178-X	_____	$9.00	_____

Crossword Omnibus Volumes
Your best puzzling values— each with 200 crosswords, at a great price!
Will Weng Sunday Crossword Omnibus

VOL	ISBN	QUANTITY	PRICE	TOTAL PRICE
1	91300-0	_____	$11.00	_____
2	91645-X	_____	$10.00	_____
3	91935-1	_____	$10.00	_____

N.Y. Times Daily Crossword Omnibus

VOL	ISBN	QUANTITY	PRICE	TOTAL PRICE
1	91094-X	_____	$10.00	_____
2	91018-4	_____	$11.00	_____
3	91066-4	_____	$10.00	_____
4	91117-2	_____	$10.00	_____
5	91708-1	_____	$11.00	_____
6	92124-0	_____	$10.00	_____
7	92541-6	_____	$11.00	_____

N.Y. Times Sunday Crossword Omnibus

VOL	ISBN	QUANTITY	PRICE	TOTAL PRICE
1	91139-3	_____	$10.00	_____
2	91791-X	_____	$10.00	_____
3	91936-X	_____	$10.00	_____
4	92480-0	_____	$11.00	_____

N.Y. Times SkillBuilder Crosswords
The first crossword series in three levels of difficulty—specially designed to teach beginners the "rules of the game" and improve puzzlers' skills.

One-star Beginner Level

VOL	ISBN	QUANTITY	PRICE	TOTAL PRICE
1	92302-2	_____	$8.00	_____
2	92305-7	_____	$8.00	_____
3	92308-1	_____	$8.50	_____

Two-star Apprentice Level

VOL	ISBN	QUANTITY	PRICE	TOTAL PRICE
1	92303-0	_____	$8.00	_____
2	92306-5	_____	$8.00	_____
3	92309-X	_____	$8.50	_____

Three-star Strategist Level

VOL	ISBN	QUANTITY	PRICE	TOTAL PRICE
1	92304-9	_____	$8.00	_____
2	92307-3	_____	$8.00	_____
3	92310-3	_____	$8.50	_____

N.Y. Times Crossword Dictionary
The revised edition of the classic reference book for crossword fans.

VOL	ISBN	QUANTITY	PRICE	TOTAL PRICE
	91131-8	_____	$21.00	_____

Acrostic Puzzles
Change-of-pace puzzles with a literary flavor that reveal interesting quotations when completed.
N.Y. Times Acrostics

VOL	ISBN	QUANTITY	PRICE	TOTAL PRICE
3	91116-4	_____	$8.50	_____
4	91302-7	_____	$8.50	_____

N.Y. Times Acrostic Omnibus

VOL	ISBN	QUANTITY	PRICE	TOTAL PRICE
3	92362-6	_____	$8.50	_____
4	92479-7	_____	$9.00	_____

L.A. Times Duo-Crostics

VOL	ISBN	QUANTITY	PRICE	TOTAL PRICE
1	92225-5	_____	$8.00	_____

GAMES Magazine Crosswords and Word Games
Lively, solver-friendly puzzles from America's most fascinating puzzle magazine.

	ISBN	QUANTITY	PRICE	TOTAL PRICE
Eyeball Benders	96366-0	_____	$14.00	_____
Paint By Numbers	92384-7	_____	$14.00	_____
World's Most Ornery Crosswords	92081-3	_____	$14.00	_____
Giant Book of Games	91951-3	_____	$14.00	_____
Will Shortz's Best Brain Busters	91952-1	_____	$12.00	_____
Games' Best Pencil Puzzles	92080-5	_____	$11.00	_____
Brain Twisters from the First World Puzzle Championships	92146-1	_____	$11.00	_____

Puzzles For Kids
Start your favorite youngster on a lifetime of brainbuilding fun! (For ages 7 to 14)

	ISBN	QUANTITY	PRICE	TOTAL PRICE
GAMES Magazine Kids' Giant Book of Games	92199-2	_____	$12.00	_____
GAMES Magazine Riddlers for Kids	92385-5	_____	$11.00	_____

Cryptic Crosswords
Sophisticated puzzles in the British style, using American English.
Random House Cryptic Crosswords

VOL	ISBN	QUANTITY	PRICE	TOTAL PRICE
1	96371-7	_____	$10.00	_____
2	92562-9	_____	$10.00	_____

GAMES Magazine Cryptic Crosswords

	ISBN	QUANTITY	PRICE	TOTAL PRICE
	91999-8	_____	$8.00	_____

N.Y. Times Puns and Anagrams

VOL	ISBN	QUANTITY	PRICE	TOTAL PRICE
1	92271-9	_____	$7.50	_____

Additional Times Books crossword puzzle books are available through your local bookstore, or fill out this coupon and return to:
RANDOM HOUSE, INC., 400 HAHN ROAD, WESTMINSTER, MD 21157. ATTN: ORDER PROCESSING

**TO ORDER CALL TOLL-FREE
1-800-793-BOOK**

☐ Enclosed is my check or money order payable to Times Books
☐ Charge my account with:　☐ American Express　☐ Visa　☐ MasterCard

[| | | | | | | | | | | | | | | | |]

EXP DATE (MO/YR)

Price applies to U.S. and territories only. In Canada write Random House of Canada, 5390 Ambler Drive, Mississauga, Ontario. (Prices subject to change.)

Please send me copies of the crossword books I have checked off, in the amounts indicated.

Name (please print) _____　Signature _____

Address _____　City _____　State _____　Zip _____

_____ Total Books
Total Dollars $ _____
Sales Tax $ _____
(Where applicable)
Postage and Handling $ **2.00**
Total Enclosed $ _____

ANSWERS

NOTE: Anagrams have been indicated by asterisks in the answer pages.

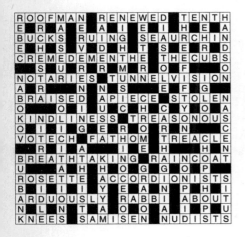

1

ACROSS: 1. RO(OF)MAN 5. RENE+WED 9. TE(NT)H* 12. BUCKetS 13. RUIN+G 14. SEA(U)RCHINg 15. C(REMEDy)EMENT+HE 16. T(H+EC)UBS 17. N+OTARIES 18. T+UN(N+ELVIS)ION 21. B+RAISED 23. A(PIE)CE 25. S+TO+LEN 28. KIND+LINES+S 30. T(REASON)O+US 32. VOTE+CH 33. FAT+HOMe 34. TREACLE* 37. BREA(THTA*)KING 39. RAINCOAT* 42. RO(SET)TE 44. (A+C+CORD)+(I+ON+IST+S) 46. eAR(DUO+US)LY 47. RA(BB)In 48. AB(O)UT 49. K+NEES (*seen* rev.) 50. SAM(IS)E+N 51. NU(DIS)TS

DOWN: 1. REBEC (hid.) 2. OR(CHEST)RA* 3. MASS+EUR (*rue* rev.) 4. NE(R)VERENDING 5. R(AIDE,)R 6. NIGHT MUSIC* 7. WE+STERN 8. DIASTOLE* 9. THR(EEF)IFTY+O+NEw (*fee* rev.) 10. NEH-RU (rev.) 11. H. AND SON 17. N(A+BOoK)OV 19. I(G+L)OO 20. N+A(U)SEA 22. SOLI+CITATIONS 24. C(H...R)OME 26. N+ASCENT 27. CART+H(AGIN+I)ANd 29. "(all-)NITRE" 31. RHINOCEROS* 35. C+HOPS,HOPS 36. AT+HEISTS 37. B(URBAN)K 38. K(HAY)+YAM 40. NONPAID* 41. G(R)ABON 43. S+IDLE 45. SITUS*

2

ACROSS: 1. ERUP+TS (all rev.) 5. VEST+A+L 9. BEFORE* 10. alEX HALEy 11. BAR+RIOt 12. BAR(FE)D 13. A+MASS 14. PIcK+A 15. LINE (hid.) 16. ALTO* 18. L+IN+K 21. HYPER+ION 23. MAS(ON)S 24. OR(N)ATE 27. BONNy 28. DURAtion 30. DENY (hid.) 31. TEN+TS (*st.* rev.) 32. ASKEW* 33. M+ORGUE* 34. I+SAId+AH 36. dOWNERS 37. FivE+RULE 38. ON(US)ES 39. C+RAN+KY

DOWN: 1. E+BB 2. REAP (hid.) 3. PORT+IA 4. TRICK+L+E 6. SH(R)ANK 7. "ALES" 8. LED (hid.) 13. mA(LIE)N 17. O(X,Y)MORON* 18. LOO+SENED* 19. S+PA+RED 20. TIN+TIN 22. ESNE* 25. G+OUD+A (all rev.) 26. TORTURE* 27. BINGES* 29. ANKARA (hid.) 33. M+OO 35. HE+Y

Unclued answers can all follow the word "cross": PATCH, BREEDING, FIRE, EXAMINE, HATCH, ROAD, BONES, DRESSER, TOWN, WALK.

3

ACROSS: 1. A(WK)WARD 7. B(RAD)Y 11. PIE(R)CE 13. tO+LIVE 15. A(TO)LL 16. AM+A+NIT+A (all rev.) 17. DO(S)ING 18. NO(HOur)W 20. pENCHANT 22. C+ANS 23. S+ALTO 25. S+LOTS 28. S+LED 30. PE(AS+AN)T 32. A(N)GRY* 34. BE(LIZ)E 36. ANDIRON* 37. AL(I)AS 38. OS+elcRIC (all rev.) 39. TR...+ALEE 40. S(N)IDE 41. KENNED+Y

DOWN: 2. WA(I)TSON 3. "KE+OGH" 4. WOR(L)D 5. GREA(S)ES* 6. DOM+IN+O 7. BLA(N)Ck 8. R+IN+G 9. DE(TEN)T (*Ted* rev.) 10. YEAST (hid.) 11. P(LA)INTS 12. CL...+OWNS 14. VI(VA+L)DI 19. bOATS 21. HAVEN (hid.) 22. C(O+W)ARDS 23. SA+LAZAR 24. O(DY)S+SEY (all rev.) 26. LEbANON 27. UNLOCK* 28. STINTER (hid.) 29. CRE(AT)ED 30. "PRAYS" 31. FAERI*+E 33. GUILEr* 34. delbBIRD (rev.) 35. ELAN (hid.)

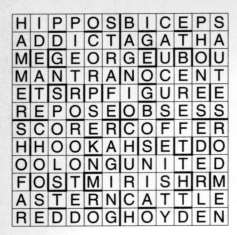

4

ANSWERS: 1. HIP+P(O)S; PIE+TRO (*ort rev.*) 2. B+ICEPS (*speci[e] rev.*); P+HONES 3. A(DDI*)CT; I'D+EATEn 4. A(GAT)HA; seCAUCUS 5. BAG+NI+O (*in rev.*); G(E)ORGE 6. CO(R)PSE; MAN+TRA (*art rev.*) 7. NO CENT; SAIUTES 8. FI(GUys)RE; STRAFE* 9. H(A+MM)ER; R(deEP)OSE 10. OBSESS*; BOSNIA (*hid. rev.*) 11. ROO(T...E)D; S+CORER 12. BERE(F)T; C+OFFER 13. HOOK+A+H; SPOOLS (*rev.*) 14. O,O+LONG; "SHOFAR" 15. RODMEN*; "U+NITED" 16. CHURCHill; M+IRISH 17. eASTERN; RA(GIN)G 18. CA+T+TLE*; FE(IST)Y 19. "CHOOSE"; REDDO+G (*odder rev.*) 20. EDERLE*; aHOY+DEN

5

ANSWERS: A. SEE(THE)D B. PRI(VA)CY C. GENERAL+GRANT D. EACH (*hid.*) E. R+OAST F. S(WEE)+TIE G. HO(O)T H. B+OU(LEVAR)D (*Ravel, duo rev.*) I. EA(S)TER J. I+DIOC(I)ESe K. NOD+DING (*don rev.*) L. I(CEHO*)+USE M. TO+UGH+IE N. S(IT)TING+PRE(T,T)Y O. OUTSIDE* P. N(EGgs)ATIVE Q. L(EEW)AY (*wee rev.*) R. Y+E(STERN)IGHT S. METE+O+RITE T. Y(OG)URT (*go rev.*) U. OGDEN NASH* V. PRice+OFFER W. I+RRE+PARABLE (*err rev.*) X. NE+PHEW Y. I+M+PET+US Z. OR(D)E+REDNESS AA. NEIGHED*

Quotation: (The movie) originally was titled *The Madness of George III*. (But) after the test screening the viewers appeared disappointed. They announced their displeasure to the producers because they "were sorry they never got around to seeing *George I* and *George II*." — S(tanley) P. Gershbein, "It's Only My Opinion"

6

ACROSS: 1. SHOT (2 defs.) 4. PUT+TEE 6. SP(R)AIN 9. C(ANT)ON 10. RO(LLI)CKING (*ill rev.*) 11. DING(H)Y 12. S...Y+Z...Y+G...Y 13. iGLOO+MY 14. CATALO+GUEs 17. S+AMPLE 20. OV(ERR)EACTS* 21. T+ISSUE 22. O+FLAT+E 25. ANSWER (*hid.*) 28. S(LOGAN)EER'S 29. CREAKY* 30. "AUGERS" 31. NO(C+EN)T 32. OLES (*hid.*) **DOWN**: 1. S(C+O)OTS* 2. H(AILS(T)OR*)MS 3. sENDING 4. PRIES(TSHI*)+P 5. T(O)PEK+A (*all rev.*) 7. P+LYING 8. R+IN+G 12. ST(A+Y)UP (*puts rev.*) 13. GRO(O)VE 14. CAROLS* 15. L(ASS)IE 16. FEmales+LICE 18. MEN+A+CEMENT 19. MI+CRO(Q)UAKE* (*I'm rev.*) 23. F(LUTE)R 24. IGN*+ORE 26. SCAR+A+B 27. D(EL)AYS 28. SANE (*hid.*)

7

ACROSS: 1. puSHY 4. W+HOPPED 6. ZORB+A (*Broz rev.*) 7. S(A+W)S 10. BEAR+D 13. O+A(K)S 15. HERB (2 defs.) 16. D(ERR)ICK 17. BUm+COLIC 19. A(FRA)ID 22. U+NITER 26. LIE (*hid.*) 27. RH(IN)O+S 28. ALTRUISM* 29. SEE+M 31. ME+LEE 32. OLE+OS (*so rev.*) 33. SNAKE (*hid. rev.*) 34. T(O)E 35. A+SP 37. ESS (*hid.*) 38. GO+O 39. TONIC (*hid.*)

DOWN: 1. S(NO)B (*all rev.*) 2. YAPS (*rev.*) 3. SH+RED 4. WOB(B)LE (*rev.*) 5. DW(A)+RF (*all rev.*) 6. Z+ERO (*ore rev.*) 8. S(K)I (*is rev.*) 9. REC(I+PI)ENT 11. ARCHI(V)E 12. DECoUPLE 14. S+CAN 15. HUN(CHE)S 17. BU(R,R)S 18. IRKS* 20. ROMULUS* 21. DEEp+MS 23. TEN (*rev.*) 24. SA(T+E)D 25. TH(RON)E 26. LI(E)NS* 30. MA+O 35. AG+O 36. POIson

Unclued answers are famous Sams: SNEAD, HOUSTON, PECKINPAH, NUNN, SHEPARD, KINISON, DONALDSON, and COOKE (as is SPADE).

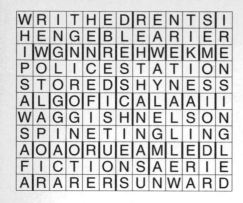

8

ACROSS: 1. WRIT+HE'D 2. RENTS (hid. rev.) 3. HENGE (hid.) 4. B(LEA)RIER 5. PO(L+ICES)TATION 6. S(TORE)+D 7. SH(YN)E+S,S (*NY* rev.) 8. W(AGG*)ISH 9. NE(L)S+ON (*sen.* rev.) 10. SPINET+IN G(L),IN G 11. FICTIONS* 12. AERIE (hid. rev.) 13. R(ARE)R 14. SU+NWARD (all rev.)

DOWN: a. W(HIPSA*),W b. S+A+FAR+I c. OPerA+L d. TO+W(E)RING e. LOG+GI+A f. C(ART)ON g. G(O)RIN+G h. THE(NC)E i. FI(ERIE)R j. OUTSIDER* k. BEDLESS* l. CHI(E)N m. S+USA+N,N+A+H n. THE(REAWA*)Y o. LE(GM)AN p. WELL (2 defs.) q. L+AN+TERN r. TIK+I (all rev.) s. EASIER* t. A(R)ID u. N(O+IS)OME v. SI(RE)N w. SING+LED

9

NINES: 1. BAN(JOEY)ES 2. CL(AMOR)ING 3. DAM+NATION 4. "EYE+BALLED" 5. IN+E+QUA(L+L)Y 6. I+N(JUST)ICE 7. JA(DEGREE)N 8. LAGNIAPPE* 9. MIN(OX)I+DIL (*lid* rev.) 10. MO(DERAT*)OR 11. O+VERSE+XED 12. PER S(EVER)E 13. PU+R+CHASER (*up* rev.) 14. REP+AIRMAN 15. SI+DE(ST)EPS (*speed is* rev.) 16. S(I+GNAT)URE

FIVES: 17. A+ITCH 18. AUDI+O 19. C+ODES 20. D(EN)IM 21. D+ROOP (*poor* rev.) 22. 'EDGES 23. GA+ZES (all rev.) 24. INDUStry 25. NADIR* 26. NO+MAD (*on* rev.) 27. O+AT+HS 28. ON-DIT* 29. RETROp (rev.) 30. SQUABbling 31. TOP+A,Z 32. U+PEN+D

10

ANSWERS: A. TEETH* B. WRA(I)TH C. O+DO+R D. WE+REWOLF (*flower* rev.) E. RIND (hid.) F. O(PHIOP*)HO+B(I)A G. N(A+Z+ARE)TH H. G(RAP)H I. SO(VIET)S J. S(ET)ATRAP K. T(I)RADE L. IP(SOFA)CTO* M. LI+FT N. LA(R)D O. D+RUGGED P. OF+F(WHIT)E Q. NAPS (rev.) R. T+W+ELVEs S. MEDI(C)ATE T. A+CORN U. KIW(AN)IS V. EYEBROWS* W. A(CC+E)PT X. RECY(C)LE* Y. I+T(C)HY Z. "GREECE" AA. HO(ME+MAD)E BB. TEN OR SO+LO

Quotation, from an item in the UK newspaper, *The Ely Standard*: "We apologize for the error in last week's paper in which we stated that Mr. Arnold Dogbody was a defective in the police force. This was a typographical error. We meant, of course, that Mr. Dogbody is a detective in the police farce."

11

ACROSS: 4. EBRO (hid.) 5. M+ANNA 6. F+ORB+I'D+S 7. MONOSKI (move *ki* from front to back of *kimonos*) 10. AC(CURS)E 11. ST(R)ANDS 13. HAVE+N 14. OSLO (hid.)

DOWN: 1. BOLd+EROS 2. BU(C+OLI*)C (*cub* rev.) 3. H+AND 8. KADDISH* 9. TU(XED)OS (*sout[h]* rev.) 12. TA(M)P

SIXES (with omissions): a. TO(ST)Y b. BOB+IN c. A+MISEr d. BE(L)AM e. SQUAd+R f. ESTER* g. BRI(H)T h. ENNA+S (*Anne* rev.) i. S(LET)S j. O+SHES k. UN(L)O+C l. AERTS* m. RAROD* n. GEIUS* o. EDITR* p. SLASH q. LOU(A)T r. EASES s. RI....+PET t. ASSES u. DALLY v. MARE+L w. ID EST x. T(A)IED y. OKAED (even letters) z. B+RAEN (*near* rev.)

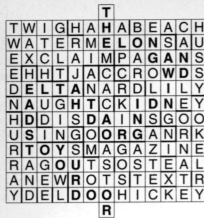

12

ACROSS: 2. T+WIG 6. tHAt+tHAt 9. B(E)ACH 13. W+A+TERM+EL+ONS* 16. EX-CLA(I)M 17. PA(GAN)S (all rev.) 21. C(ROW)DS 22. DEL+T+A (all rev.) 24. NAR+D (all rev.) 25. LI'L+Y 26. NAUGHTy 28. KID+NEY (yen rev.) 31. D+ISDA*+INS 32. GO+O 34. U+SING 35. O+RGAN* 37. TOnYS 41. MA+GAZ(IN)E 45. R(AGO)UTS 47. O+STEAL 48. ANEW (hid.) 49. ROTS (hid.) 50. T(E+X),T 51. DO+O+HICK+EY (ye rev.)

DOWN: 1. THEM (hid.) 2. T(W)EED 3. WAX (2 defs.) 4. pITCH 5. GE(L)T 7. AM I 8. ALP (hid.) 9. BOARDING* 10. ENG+OLDS 11. CAN(D+L)E 12. H(US)SY* 14. RA(JA)HS 15. S(A)WING 18. HE+ADS+T+AND 19. ANTDOM (hid.) 20. C+A+C+A+O 23. LUD (hid.) 27. G+IN 28. KIR (hid.) 29. YOK(EL)R*+Y 30. HURR(A)Y 33. OR(N)ATE 36. A+Z+TEC 38. OGE+E (ego rev.) 39. Y+OWL 40. SU...RD 42. A+STORe 43. GOSH* 44. ASTIr 46. T+O-O

13

ACROSS: 2. VI(T)AL 6. LEAN (2 defs.) 10. CO(AS)T 25. PRE(STUD)Y 26. D(I)OR (rev.) 27. LI(M)PS 28. "SEE" 29. O+N(L)Y 30. A+S+PIC 31. TAR HEEL* 33. "REDDY" 34. S+YRIA (airy rev.) 36. O(W)N 37. LIGHT (acronym) 40. PUT (hid.) 41. VICE (2 defs.) 42. "CUE" 44. ROPE (hid.) 45. AR(MLE)TS* (elm rev.) 46. W R A P

DOWN: 4. bIRd+IS+H 5. ASPIRINg 12. fOYER 15. DO+T 20. AD+O 21. SINE DIE* 23. TO+LEDO ([m]odel rev.) 24. "WRYLY" 25. P(L)AYS 32. HER+R 33. R+APT 35. YE+W 37. L(EVE)E 38. G(UL...)AG 39. HE+ART 40. P+OWER 43. E.T.A.

Unclued answers are 15 of the cards in a tarot deck indicated by their designated numbers.

14

ANSWERS: 1. EASY (hid.) 2. PAL+M 3. ON+C...E 4. SU(R)E 5. U(BANG)+I 6. F. LEE 7. F(A)UN+A; FESS (hid.) 8. BELL+A 9. A+P+ED 10. INVADE* 11. M(ERR)Y 12. MA(N)X 13. SIGN+OR 14. O+LIVER 15. sinGL(IMPS)ES 16. SAV(AG)E 17. L+OVER 18. VER+SU+S (all rev.) 19. HE+L+L 20. PA(M)PA'S; POLK+AS 21. BU(D)S 22. HE(A)RS 23. CHILd+I 24. N(hOBO+D)Y; NOCTU*+RN 25. COR+PS (roc rev.) 26. UP(O)N 27. AUDI+O 28. wHO'S+ANNA 29. LI(E)D 30. DRAG+ON 31. sUPPER 32. BALl+I 33. KISS (hid.); K(ITBA*)G 34. DUAL (rev.) 35. SO+PRA*+NO 36. "NO+AH" 37. DEVIL (rev.) 38. HIS+PANIC 39. S+PIT 40. I+M+PEACH; tISSUE 41. TINKER (rev.) 42. ALl+IT; AV(O)ID 43. L+EASE 44. T+ENTH*

Border letters spell (*Northern*) *Exposure*, (*Eastern*) Airlines, (*southern*) hospitality, (*western*) movie.

15

ANSWERS: A. S(WEE)Py B. TONI*+C C. BANNER (2 defs.) D. COCO+ON E. BLITHER (2 defs.) F. C+LIMBER G. COT+TONY H. GARBLESs I. P(ON)+TIFF J. RACI(E)ST K. RAD(I)OED (deodar rev.) L. SELE(CT)S M. S+UNLESS N. CLI(N)CHED O. F(OL)LOWER (lo rev.) P. "KAMIK+AZE" Q. P(ROB)+ABLY R. BO(WANDA)RROW S. CAN+D(L)ELIGHT T. O(MARK+HAY)YAM (mayo rev.) U. SA+GITTARIUS* V. TEMPERA+MEN+T W. C+ON+T(ROVERS)IES

Additional clues: 1. Wizardry shown by soldier wearing raincoat [MA(GI)C] 2. Piece of broccoli found in assistant's stomach [A(B)IDE] 3. Some people might've sent back letter [GIMEL (hid. rev.)] 4. Model airplane's tail taken by one backward boy [I+D(E)AL (lad rev.)] 5. Returning collect calls for orchestra member [CELLO (hid. rev.)]

16

ACROSS: 1. "SEQ+UIN" 5. R(EL)ENT 10. RACe+IN 12. MID+ST (dim rev.) 13. GAB ON 14. SA(C)+KING 15. CO(LORE)D 17. PRO+JE(C)T+ED 18. CORNEAm* 20. PRE-Z 23. NE+ON ([m]en rev.) 25. ODESSA (hid. rev.) 27. D(ETO*)URING 32. FR+ANTIC 33. AN(YBO*)D+Y 34. OD+DER (all rev.) 35. S(TOW*)S 36. HO...AX 37. SK(IMP)Y 38. pRELATE

DOWN: 1. GO(UN)OD 2. CAIRN (move *i* in *car in*) 3. NO+N(A+G)O+N 4. B(OJ)ANGLES 5. CA+NINE 6. SHE(PAR)D 7. AND+crESts 8. CO(L)T 9. KAREEM* 11. IRED* 16. STI+E+GLITZ (*it's* rev.) 19. DO(YEN)NE 21. FO(X+T+R)OT 22. SIR+UP+Y 24. K+I+DNA+P (*and I* rev.) 26. AD(ORE)D 28. PIV+OT (all rev.) 29. N+YET 30. HEA(R)D 31. MOBS (hid.)

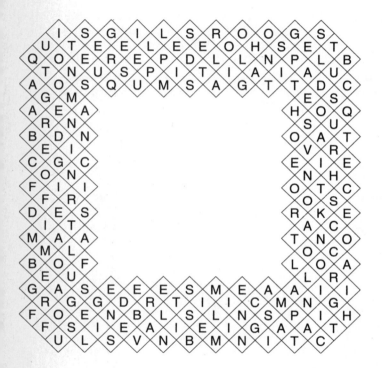

17

ANSWERS: 1. NOT(QUIT)E 2. TON(SURE)S 3. S(QUEEG)EE 4. SUPP(LI)ER 5. I+M+P(EL)LED 6. E+PI(ST)LES 7. TAILORED* 8. HO(OLI*)GAN 9. HO'S+P(IT)AL 10. GELATINS* 11. BU(D+APES)T 12. MEGATONS* 13. O+S+CU+LATE 14. DRAGO(MA)N 15. SQUA(SHE)D 16. BEG+INNER 17. VIRTUOSO (hid. rev.) 18. COIN-CIDE 19. T+HE(R)AVEN 20. OFF(ER)ING 21. CHINO(OK)S 22. FIR+STAID 23. ANCESTOR (hid.) 24. I+M+MOL(A+T)E 25. COCK+AT+O,O 26. F(LAM)+BEAU 27. CA(RIng)LL ON 28. GORGE+Of+US 29. OR(I+GIN)AL 30. SU(FF+RAG)E 31. GO+SLINGS 32. B(ESIE*+G)ED 33. LA+VENDER 34. BAN(I'S)TER 35. LI+BEL(IS)T 36. MIN(I+M+IS)E 37. C(EI)LINGS (*i.e.* rev.) 38. CAMP+AIGN* 39. T(A'S)+MANIA 40. NIGH+TCAP (*pact* rev.)

18

ACROSS: 4. CAT+SUP; SC...+OR...+CH...; SPACER* 7. A(GELE*)SS; E(CLIPS),E; ENDEARS* 9. ATTUNED*; EXUL(T)ED (rev.); PRI(V+I)ES 10. HOL(YOK)E; O(D,D)NE+SS; SQUA(RE)D 11. AB'S+T+AIN*; A(LAB)+AMA; IMMERSE (hid.) 12. A(R+TWO)RK; BUL(WAR)K; I+BE+RIANt 13. ADD(RES)S; GRI(EVE)D; SN(OR)K(E)L 14. E(I)THER; MO(N)TEL; ST(R)AYS

DOWN: 1. HEDONISM*; P+AS+SABLE; RE(D+HE)ADS 2. B(L)UDGE+ON; DE+C+UP+LET; I DO+LATER 3. A+P+PETITE; DEC(R)EASE; TAX+ON+O+MY 5. A+GITATOR (*rotati[n]g* rev.); CLUB'S+ODA (*ado* rev.); PO(T)EM+KIN 6. CON+G+REVE (*ever* rev.); RE(TRAC)ED (*cart* rev.); SKIM+ASKS 8. E+A+SING; SEDAKA (hid.); S(PEAK),S

19

ANSWERS: A. CRY+P+T B. UNLIT* C. W+ENDS D. C(RUT)+CH E. HUMPTY* F. MET+HOD G. W+HOOPS H. RE(E)NTER I. SO+OTHER J. WA(IF+I)SH K. BURG+LARS L. TE+THE RED (*E.T.* rev.) M. T+HAIL+AND N. THOU+SAND O. DU(CHESS)ES* P. "SOME+WHERE" Q. SYN+THE+SIZES (*NYS* rev.) R. IMPRI(SON+ME)NT S. M+ATHEMATICAL T. CL(IN+TEAS+TWO)OD U. S(T)REETS+WEEPER (*steers* rev.) V. Z(I+P+A+DEED)OO+DAH (*had* rev.)

Quotation: Yes, it's true that I don't do crossword puzzles. The first one I tried, many years ago . . . stumped me with the clue "Charles Lamb's pen name." . . . So did the second. When that same clue showed up in the third, I threw the newspaper across the room. — Calvin Trillin

20

ACROSS: 2. M(ORT)AR 7. VI+SAS 12. P+Of+PUP 14. D+I(MME'S)T 16. "ERE" 18. AP(A+C)E 19. A(PR)IL 20. BEGONIA* 22. S(I+L)OS 26. "GAITERS" 29. sAVANT 30. DR+ESDEN* 33. CA+T(A)RACT 35. B(I)DE* 36. "KNEW" 39. SHRE(W)D 42. T+OAST+Y 43. lURCHINg 44. D+ELTA* 45. LE(A)+KING

DOWN: 1. S+PEAK 2. M(O...R)PH 3. OP(E)RAh 4. RUB+I+CON 5. A+D+S 6. RISEN* 8. I+M+POSTS 9. SEANCE* 10. AS+CII 11. S(TEAK),S 22. SACKS (2 defs.) 23. IVANHOE* 24. LATER+goAL 27. ARCHer 28. R(E)DSKIN* 31. D+IE 32. N,E,W,S 34. TETRA (2 defs.) 37. WE+ST 40. S(U)...E 41. CHI (hid.)

Theme Words are the Three Little Pigs' building materials; with their Variations, they are: STRAW (BOSS, POLL [two-word phrases]), STICKS (CLINGS, ADHERES [synonyms]), BRICK (MAGGIE, BIG DADDY [characters from *Cat on a Hot Tin Roof*]).

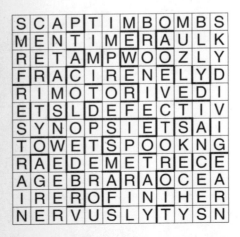

21

ANSWERS: 1. DEB+RIS (both rev.) 2. IN+STEP (*pets* rev.) 3. GR+AB 4. cASH 5. STEER (2 defs.) 6. A+P(E)RY 7. CA(IS+SO)N 8. A(DJ+OUR)N 9. EINSTEIN* 10. IC(H)ING 11. DIME (hid.) 12. CRE(MAT)ED 13. singERIN 14. GANG (2 defs.) 15. IR(A+Q)IS 16. JIM(MY)I+soNG 17. AERO (hid. rev.) 18. IS+R+A+ELIS 19. ON(TAR)IOn 20. E(MM)YS* 21. BOy+REAL 22. VI(S)I+ON 23. KE(L,L)Y 24. DES+K'S 25. PAU*+LINE; PU+MA (*up* rev.) 26. ME+SOMORP+HOUSe (*promos* rev.) 27. QUA(R+TERM)ILER 28. I(T)CH 29. LA(ST)ED (*deal* rev.) 30. MAD At ME; M(A)E 31. NIM (hid.) 32. DOME(STI)+CABLE (*it's* rev.) 33. LIBido 34. B(ARE+L)Y 35. LI+NEAR 36. RAINS (2 defs.) 37. D(EL)IVERS (*le...* rev.); DORSAL (hid.) 38. CU+E 39. G,A,B,B,E,D 40. S'AD (rev.); SI(G)N 41. GA+MS 42. SATE (2 defs.) 43. HOLY (hid.) 44. IO(WAs)N 45. W+RAP (all rev.) 46. ANI (hid.) 47. EACH (hid.) 48. "CEES"

22

Omitted letters are given in brackets.

ACROSS: 1. S+C[R]AP 4. T+IM[E]BOMBS* 10. ME[A]N+TIME* 11. [C]AU(L)K 12. RETA[G] (hid.) 13. WO(OZ)[I]LY* 14. C[A]+IRENE 16. [T]R(I'M)OTOR 17. VE[R]DI* 18. D+EFE(C)T*+I+V[E] 20. S'YNOP+SI[Z]+E (all rev.) 24. TO WE[D] 26. SPOO(K)[I]N+G 28. DE(MET)[E]R 31. A[L]GE+BRA 32. O+CEA[N]* 33. [H]IRER 34. FIN(I[S]+H)ER 35. N+ER(V)[O]USLY* 36. TYS[O]N (hid.)

DOWN: 1. S[M[U]R]F 2. C(E'[L]ER)ITY 3. [B]ANT(AM)S 4. TI M'I[D] (all rev.) 5. I'M+PRO[V]+E 6. BR(O[W]N)IE 7. MU(Z)[Z]LE 8. B[E](L,L)Y 9. SK(Y)DI*+VI[N]+G 14. COL(O[R]+E)D 15. EV[I]CTOR* 16. REST+RAIN[T] 19. [F]IANCEES* 21. PTEROU[S]* 22. I[M]P+ERIL (all rev.) 23. S+KE[T](CH)Y 25. WEE[P]-ER 27. AGRE[E]* 29. T+A[W]NY 30. [Y]EARN

Poser: What entry in every crossword puzzle would be a palindrome if its first letter were changed?
Answer: "Two down"

23

ACROSS: 1. CARBO(H)Y+D+RATE 11. GOLFS (acronym) 13. HI(L)D+A 15. NOT IF+Y 16. DO(CT)OR 17. TeRAGIC (rev.) 18. ELKO 19. O(A+T)H 20. COLE+USES 22. UBER* 25. PE(N)STER 28. RENO 31. R+AIDS 32. EVE (2 defs.) 33. G+RASP 34. ELY 36. DEW (hid.) 37. IN+TAG+LIO (oil gat rev.) 39. SEPTILLION* 41. SELMA* 44. Y+OWL* 46. SAKE (2 defs.) 47. BEA(U+VOId)R 48. G+REENS (sneer rev.) 50. E(NGAG*)+E 51+52+53. TASSEL*

DOWN: 1. C(ONTO)URED 2. AGORA (2 defs.) 3. ROT+ATE 4. BLIGHt 5. OFF,ICE 6. Y+O+DELERS 7. D+HOLE 8. RICKover 9. ALTOS (hid.) 10. EARLS (even letters) 12. S(YCOP*)HAN'T 14. DO+NEES (seen rev.) 21. US+IN+G 23. B+E(V)EL 24. ROG(U)ER+Y 26. NA(PAL)M 27. RAY+ON 29. NEWSY (hid. rev.) 30. GRIPe 34. ELI(Z)A 35. LI(ON)KING 38. TI(LLA)GEr (all rev.) 40. LAS VEGAS 41. SOBer 42. dEWES (rev.) 43. V+ERSE 45. BUR(N)T 49. EASELp*

Diagram outline resembles map of Nevada.

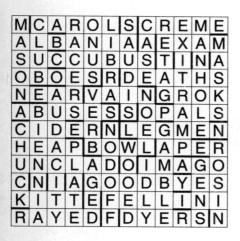

24

ANSWERS: 1. AL(BAN)IA; C(L)UB; M+AS+ON 2. CAR+OLd; L(I)+BRA; ON US 3. CREME (hid. rev.); R(ET)AG; SUCCUmB+US 4. E+XAM (max rev.); M(AN+H)OLE; M+ASKS 5. A(BUS)ES (all rev.); BIEN+NI+A (in rev.); hOBOES 6. NEAR (hid.); "RA+CER'S"; VA(I)N 7. CASE*; GR+OK; SAUDIS* 8. D+EAT(H)S; EX(I)-TRAMP; O+PAL'S 9. AUD(A+C)IT+Y; HE(A)P; lUNCh+LAD 10. CIDE*+R; P+LATE; VERB (hid.) 11. BOWL (2 defs.); I'M+A+G+O; NOvEL 12. APER (hid.); LEG(ME)N*; ROSIN* 13. CHUCK (2 defs.); KIT+T; RAYED* 14. A(GE)D; GO(ODBY*)ES; NOD OFF* 15. G+AMBLE; solIDLY; WO+OED 16. D(Y)ER+S (red rev.); FELL IN+I; GENS (odd letters)

25

ANSWERS: 1. WE+A+K 2. HO(Y)LE 3. TWIN+E 4. B+I(KIN)I 5. FAT+HOMe 6. F+LIGHT 7. FUTURE (last letters) 8. H+EIGHT 9. T+WITCH 10. W(IT)+HI+N 11. TWE*+L+FT+H 12. FRES+H(M)EN (serf rev.) 13. H(ELPMA)TE* (ample rev.) 14. MA+T+A+HAR+I (all rev.) 15. ME ANTI ME 16. T(WINK)IES 17. WHEELING (2 defs.) 18. W(HIT)E+SO+X 19. MOONSHINE* 20. NAUGHT+IE+R 21. S(I+MOLE)ONS 22. SQUAW+KING 23. T+RIMESTER 24. DIAP+H(AN)OUSe (paid rev.) 25. REGEN(ERA)CY 26. THUMBELINA* 27. C(ONSIDE*)RATE 28. LOO(SELIP)PED (piles rev.)

Verse reads down the first column, then up the second, down the third, etc.: There once was a poet named Knight / Whose limericks weren't quite right. / His rhyming was fine / Until the fifth line. / Then he always managed to bollix it up somehow.

26

ACROSS: 8. M+AGOG 12. AGAVE (hid.) 14. auSTRIA 15. B+IS ON 16. LA(R)GER 17. eARTh 18. FI(LAME+N)T 20. L+rOYALTY 23. SPAN-ISH 26. A(M)BLE 29. S(NOt)OP 31. PRO (odd letters) 32. EL+LA 33. PIET+A 34. BOy+A 35. TH(RE)E 36. AGREES* 37. DO+E 38. EDDY*

DOWN: 1. FISCAL (hid.) 2. ANTH(R+OP)OLOGY 3. RA(R+IT)Y 4. M+AILMAN* 5. EGA+D (all rev.) 6. nRA+BB+IT'S 7. EVen+ILLY 8. MESA (hid.) 9. GINGERBREAD* 10. O+F+TENS 11. G+EAR 13. W+OR+M 18. F+L+INCHED 19. TE(E+NAG)E 21. NAPPED (2 defs.) 22. UM+P+IRE 24. A+G...L+ARE 25. HOT+EL 27. L+O(T,T)O 28. DE(B)AR 29. SA(T+E)D 30. sOARS

Unclued entries are FARMER, WIFE, CHILD, NURSE, DOG, CAT, RAT, and of course the CHEESE stands alone.

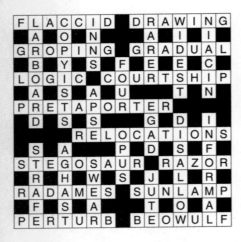

27

ACROSS: a. LOG+IC b. "RAZOR" c. B(EOW)ULF (all rev.) d. DRA(WIN)G e. FLAC+CID (calf rev.) f. GR+A+DUAL (all rev.) g. GRO(P+IN)G h. PERTUR*+B i. RAn+DAMES j. SU(NLAM*)P k. COU(RTSHI*)P l. ST(EGOS+A)UR (ruts rev.) m. P+RE(T+A)PORTER n. REL(OC)ATIONS (co. rev.)

DOWN: 1. LAR(BOAR)D 2. COP(Y+IST)S 3. IN+N+S 4. RA(R)ER (rear rev.) 5. W+ID EST 6. NIAC+IN (Cain rev.) 7. "FOUR" 8. collAPSE 9. EGA+D (all rev.) 10. DI+SALLOW (I'd rev.) 11. INFORM+A+L 12. OPUS* 13. STRAFE* 14. AGHA+ST 15. aS WE ARe 16. JUT+E

28

ANSWERS: 1. AVERS+ANT 2. S+CAN 3. MASS+AC(HUSET*)T+SANS 4. RAGS (hid.) 5. SILO (hid.) 6. OVER (hid.) 7. ACES* 8. TE(A)M (Met rev.) 9. SAGE (hid.) 10. GAM+E 11. DE(L)L (rev.) 12. LIED (2 defs.) 13. A+COL(Y+T)E'S 14. M+AR(SEILLA)ISE (Allies rev.) 15. DO+L+L 16. P(E+RSEVE*)RANCE 17. T(EX),T 18. oLOGY 19. COUNT+ERC(LOCK)WISE* 20. C(HER)OKE+E 21. U+N(WI(E)LD)Y 22. A+N(T)EATER 23. J(OK)E 24. E+RRS 25. VAN+E 26. RENT (2 defs.) 27. K+L+ON(DIK)E (kid rev.) 28. DI(N)G 29. SEVE(NTEEN(HUN)D*)RED 30. OVERRODE (hid. rev.) 31. A(NT)E 32. N+IN+O 33. K(NO)C+KING 34. RESPON(SELES)S* 35. CONSPIRE* 36. O(P)EC* 37. KUHN* 38. JARS (2 defs.) 39. MO(RTA*)LLY 40. YE+L,L 41. THE(A+T)+ROMANIA 42. gREEK 43. "SIZE" 44. "HEAL" 45. IR(K)S

29

ACROSS: 1. RAFTER (hid. rev.) 7. A+DU(L)TS (stud rev.) 12. B+A+THING 13. GO+Y+I'M 14. WO+M+BAT 15. IC+ECAPS (all rev.) 16. ULNA (hid.) 17. G(A)LOP 18. A+F(GH)AN 20. MO(ROC+C)O 23. E+JE(C)T+O+R 27. S+CUL(P)T 30. S(AB)OT 31. DUCK (2 defs.) 32. C(OVER)UP 34. C(OWB*)OY 35. MIGHT (2 defs.) 36. S(A+H)ARAN 37. X(ER)X'ES 38. OFF+ICE

DOWN: 1. S(L)IGHT 2. BAN(ACE)K 3. DA(W+D)LE 4. VEGA* 5. D+YNA+ST (any D rev.) 6. S(A+SS)OON 8. EV(OK)E 9. TIN+TIN+G 10. K(HA)K+I 11. SI+T+CO+M (is rev.) 19. WA(LLAB)Y (ball rev.) 21. O(PIe)NION 22. CAN'T+IN+A 23. DR(EAR)Y 24. G(RUN)GE (egg rev.) 25. JA(PIN)G 26. O+USTED 28. T+AXIS 29. RI(N)SE 33. F(IV)E

30

ANSWERS: A. VAN(QU)ISH B. EB+BING (*be* rev.) C. RE(JO+I)NDER D. SQUASH (2 defs.) E. EARTHWARD* F. BUT+AN+E G. YELL+O+WISH H. SINCE+RELY I. T(WEED+LED)EE J. EF(FOR)T K. P(ROTE)+STATION L. "HIGHLY" M. ELBOW (*wob[b]le* rev.) N. NECKER+CHIEF O. S+CH(N+ORR)ER P. OW(N)ED Q. N(ON)PR+OF+IT R. D(RUN)+KEN S. HUgo+F(FISH)LY T. EYEFULo* U. I+NEAR+NEST V. MON(K)EY

Quotation: Fair Brooklyn / Pride of the Port of New York / There's a friendly golf course with greens / And a friendly hash house with beans / There's a friendly clink whence come juvenile delinquents / But they were born in Queens. — Verse by Stephen Sondheim

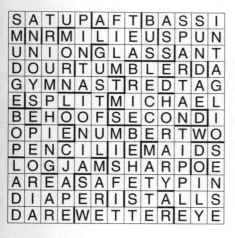

GAELIC	GLACIER	CLEARING	N R
TIRING	IGNITER	INTRIGUE	E U
SECANT	ASCENTS	NEWSCAST	W S
GERBIL	GILBERT	BLIGHTER	T H
O'LEARY	LOYALER	ALLEGORY	G L
REMAND	AMERIND	MERIDIAN	I I
REASON	ENAMORS	NORSEMAN	N M
LEADER	REGALED	BELGRADE	G B
SIGNET	SEATING	TANGIERS	R A
MANGER	REAMING	GERANIUM	I U
BARBIE	GABBIER	CRIBBAGE	C G
RUSSET	RESHUTS	THRUSHES	H H

31

SIXES: 1. GAELIC (*E* for *L* in *Gaelic*) 2. TIe+RING 3. S(E)CANT 4. G+ERBIL (*libre* rev.) 5. O+LEARY* 6. RE(MAN)D 7. RE+A+SON 8. LE+A+DER (all rev.) 9. SIGNET* 10. M+ANGER 11. BAR(BI....)E 12. Rice+US+SET

SEVENS: a. AME(RI)ND b. AS(CENT)S c. ENAMORS* d. G+ABB(IE)R e. G+I(LB'ER)T f. G+LACIER g. dIG+NITER h. LO(YALE)Rd i. RE+AMI+NG j. RE(GAL)ED k. RESHUTS* l. S+EATING

EIGHTS: m. ALL(E)+GORY n. BE+L(GRAD)E o. B+LIGHTER p. CL(EAR)ING q. CRIBBAGE* r. G(E+RANI)UM s. IN+TR(IG)UE (*GI* rev.) t. MERIDIAN* u. N+EWSCAST* v. NOR+SEMAN (all rev.) w. TANGIER+S x. THRU+SHES

32

ACROSS: 1. S(A)TUP (*puts* rev.) 5. A+FT 8. BASSI (hid. rev.) 13. M(I+LIE)Ud 14. UN(I)ON (*non-U* rev.) 16. AN+T 17. D+OUR 20. RED TAG* 22. MICHAEL* 24. BE+HOOF 25. O+PIE 30. M(AID)S 33. nosLO+G+JAM (all rev.) 36. AR...EA 39. STALLS (2 defs.) 40. D(A)R+E 41. WE(T,T)ER* 42. EYE (hid.)

DOWN: 1. S+MUD+GE (*e.g.* rev., & lit.) 2. "A+NNOYS" 3. T(R(I)UMP)HING 4. PIN+TA (*at* rev.) 6. eFIL+M (all rev.) 7. TEAm 8. B+US 9. AS+S 10. SP(ART)AN 11. SUNDAncE 12. INT(A)GLIO* 13. "MORN" 15. G(US+T)FUL* 18. BR...IE 19. L+ECCE 21. IO(N)I+A 23. HORARY* 24. BOP (2 defs.) 26. PEOR(I)A* 27. MIS(F+I)T 28. BE(HE)ST 29. TI(PP)LE 30. MA(T)TE 31. D+OILY 32. SENSEn 33. LAD+D 34 J+APE 35. MA...RE 37. EAR (hid.) 38. SEW (hid.)

Chain, from TOP to BOTTOM, reads: TOP, SPUN, GLASS, TUMBLER, GYMNAST, SPLIT, SECOND, NUMBER TWO, PENCIL, SHARP, SAFETY PIN, DIAPER, BOTTOM.

33

ANSWERS: 1-19. SE(N)AT+OR 2-31. BR(END)A 3-27. S+EVEN 3-31. B+OAR(D)S 4-25. DA(SHE)D 5-44. R(E)N+OWNED 5-57. HEAVE+NWARD (*drawn* rev.) 6-15. WOLF* 6-35. BE(L)LOW 7-26. CARSon 7-30. S+PAWN 8-36. WO(ODE)N 9-34. BRAWNY (*W* for *I* in *brainy*) 10-11. DAM (hid.) 10-20. A+RM 12-17. AD+I+T 13-26. CA+PER 14-29. N(E)AP (rev.) 14-46. PAC(K)ERS 16-24. PO(LIT)E 16-37. SCAM+P 18-48. VER(BE)NA* 19-51. SHE+BEEN 21-38. MICA (hid.) 21-60. MAN-EATER* 22-34. "WRIGLEY" 23-25. D(O+GM)ATA 25-68. CONVERTED* 28-63. TAN GENT 32-73. FRIEDM(A)No* 33-55. SA+R+DINE 34-76. B(OUNDAR*)Y 35-66. BRA(V)ADO* 36-59. L+EARN 38-42. AN(NET)TE 39-46. STRAND (2 defs.) 39-72. DRA(STI)C (all rev.) 40-54. GEES+E 41-72. ELASTIC (hid. rev.) 43-75. RE(E)NTER 45-78. O(C+TAnk)NE 46-77. WHINES* 47-50. DE(IS)M 49-71. pinTER+MS 52-74. TH(R)EE 53-71. V+ENDORSe 56-64. S(PA)TS 58-79. S(H)UN 59-78. LO(C)O 60-75. ROO(S)TER 61-77. ARROW* 62-67. CO(E)D 64-74. S+TAT(U)E 65-69. R+I+ME 70-76. BEASTIE*

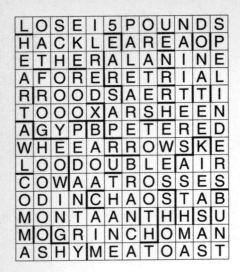

34

ACROSS: 1. LOSE 15 POUNDS 11. HACK+L+E 13. AREA (hid.) 14. ETHER* 15. ALA+NINE 16. A+FOR+E 19. RETRIAL* 20. RO(O)DS 22. AL(B)ERT 23. TOO(L)B+O,X (all rev.) 24. A+R+SHEEN 26. GYP (acronym) 29. PETE+RED 32. W+HEEL+BAR+ROWS 36. L+O,O 37. "DOUB'LE" 39. A-I+R 40. COWorkers 41. A+L(BAT+R)OSSES 43. O+DIN 44. CHA(O)Se 46. TAB (hid.) 48. MONT(ALB*)ANa 50. GRIN+C+H 51. OMAN (hid.) 52. A+SHY 53. M(ELBAT)+OAST (table rev.)

DOWN: 2. O+AT 3. SCHO(O+L+B)OY* 4. EKE (hid.) 5. I'LL+B(R)E+D 6. P(ALLB*+EAR)ER 7. Of+RATES 8. NAIL-BITERS* 9. DON(ATE*)E 10. SPE(LLBI*)NDERS 11. HEART* 12. EAR (hid.) 17. FRO+G 18. ROOm 21. SAP (hid.) 25. "AWL" 27. PEDANTRY* 28. B+A+L+BOA 30. TO (L,L) BOOT+H 31. EWES (hid.) 33. HOOD(O,O)S 34. EL+Bus+OWING 35. KIEL*+BAS(A)S 38. B+RAN+CA 39. ASk THe MAn 40. CO(M)MA 42. TH(AN)E 45. SHOO (move *H* in *SoHo*) 47. BU(N)T 49. AIM*

35

ANSWERS: A. W(O,O)+DC)HOPPER B. IN(DI)VISIBILITY C. L+ADS D. LO(OK'ING)G+LASS E. I'M+M(UNIT)Y F. AN,THE+M G. MO+'UNTED H. S+CHENE(C+TAD)Y I. AU(TO+E)Di J. FOOTNOTE (hid. rev.) K. IG+LOOSe (*GI* rev.) L. RU(TAB+A)G+A M. ECTOPLASMIC* N. FUR ROW O. UPHOL(ST)ERY* P. MOO+C+HER Q. BUTCHERS* R. LE(WIt)S S. E(COFRE*)+AK T. RA(BB+I)T (all rev.) U. UNWIELD*+Y V. L+IF+TOFF W. E(STAB+L+IS)H (*he* rev.) X. S(WEE+T+T)OOTH

Quotation: Many of us like to stretch the minds of our readers, introducing them to the big menu behind the list of daily word specials, but all too often we practice polysyllabicism because we want to show off. Lookame, I got this prodigious vocabulary. — William Safire, *Fumblerules*

36

SEVENS: 1. AN+TONY+M 2. A+SE(X+U)AL 3. A+SHIEST 4. E+UP+HE+MY 5. E(X)HAUST* 6. FIEL+DER (all rev.) 7. G+UTTERS 8. H+O(STES)S (all rev.) 9. M(ATIN*+E)E 10. NOTICES (*T* for *V* in *novices*) 11. O+RIF+ICE (*fir* rev.) 12. P(A+JAM)A'S 13. P(IN)B+ALL 14. RE+T+OUCH 15. REVOL+V...E (*lover* rev.) 16. TERM+I+N+I

EIGHTS: 17. C+ASH*+MERE 18. DECI+S+I'VE (*iced* rev.) 19. EPITAPHS* 20. VER(BALL)Y

NINES: 21. BA(THRO)BES 22. C+OFFERING 23. CONSULTED* 24. DAIQU*+IRIS 25. FOR(EAR)MED 26. F(RAG)RANCE 27. I+DENT(I+C)AL 28. J(AUNT+I)EST 29. MARQUE(T+T)E 30. M(EYE)R+BEER 31. P(A+RAT+R)OOP 32. POUR+BO(I)RE 33. REPR(I)EVES* 34. S(EDI(MEN)T)S (*tide* rev.) 35. V(EL+VET)EE+N 36. YAP(P+I+NES)S (all rev.)

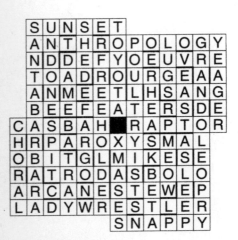

37

ANSWERS: 1. "CHORAL"; S(NAP)PY; SUNSET*; YEA(GE)R (*e.g.* rev.) 2. A(NTHRO*)POLOGY; G(RANDOLE*)O+PRY; LAD+Y(W+REST)LER (*rely* rev.); S(ANT+A+BAR,BAR)A 3. DEF+Y; EAST (hid.); SPIT (rev.); STEW (hid.) 4. AR(CAN)E; AS(LEE)P; OEUVRE (*Eve* alternated with *our*); UNDONE (hid.) 5. BO(L)O; L+U(G)S; TO+AD; TRA+Y (*art* rev.) 6. DAM+E (*mad* rev.); M+EOW (*woe* rev.); TRO+D (all rev.); URGE (hid.) 7. A+R+GO; ME+ET; MI...KE; RHEA* 8. BE-TA (half rev.); O+BIT; SA(N)G; S(HE)D 9. BE(dEFEAT)ERS; FREEH+OLDER; PA+ROXY+SMALl; PO(rUm)L+TRY(I)ST 10. CAS(BA)H; RAPTOR*; TO(Y)OT+A; X+MASES (*sesam[e]* rev.)

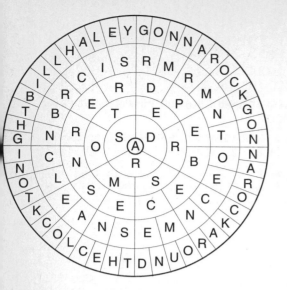

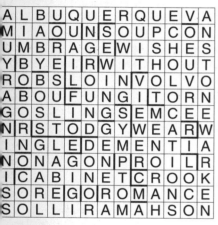

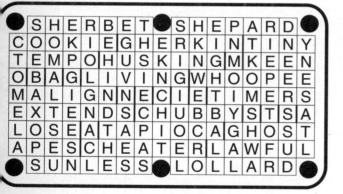

38

ANSWERS: 1. G+R(AD)ED 2. DE(O+D)AR (*D O* rev.) 3. MADDEN (2 defs.) 4. D+AM+NED (all rev.) 5. PAR+AD+E 6. DR+APER 7. POt+MADE 8. CA(M)PE+D 9. D(ARK)EN 10. G+ARDEN 11. expectORATED 12. AR(D)EN'T 13. BRAND+O 14. A+B+ROAD 15. "BARRED" 16. B(O)READ 17. SCAR(C)E 18. SAC(K)ER* 19. A+RENAS (*saner* rev.) 20. S+NARER (*reran* rev.) 21. MARC(O)S (*scram* rev.) 22. S(A)CRUM 23. C(R)ANES 24. S(ACRE)D 25. ST(R)EAM 26. HAREMS* 27. MEANER (2 defs.) 28. CAR MEN 29. ALA(RM)S 30. AROMAS (acronym) 31. SC(RE)AM 32. MAKE(R)S* 33. TALONS* 34. S(A+LO)ON 35. C(ANON)'S 36. C+AS+IN+O 37. OR+GANS (*snag* rev.) 38. SHAR+ON (*rahs* rev.) 39. T(AB)ORSo 40. ABSORB (hid.) 41. SATI(R)E 42. wALTERS 43. CAST+LE 44. SCAT+HE 45. TIARASe* 46. T(R)AILS 47. A(S+SE)RT 48. "SATYRS"

Outer circle reads "Gonna rock, gonna rock, around the clock tonight." — Bill Haley

39

ACROSS: 9. M+I(A)OU 10. SO(UP+C)ON 12. UMBR(AG)E* (*GA* rev.) 14. W+I+SHES 15. B(Y)E 16. WI(THOU)T 17. ROBS (hid. rev.) 19. LOIN (odd letters) 20. V+O(LV)O 21. ABOUt 23. FUN+GI 24. T...O+R...N 25. GO+SLINGS 27. EM,CEE 29. STO(D)GY 31. W(E)AR 32. sINGLE 35. DE(MEN+T)IA* 36. N(ON)AG+ON 38. bROIL 40. CABINET* 41. C+ROOK 42. S+ORE 43. ROMANCE (acronym)

DOWN: 1. LIMB+O 2. BA(B)Y 3. "QUAIL" 4. U+NG+ROUND 5. R+OWING 6. QUITo 7. UPSHOT* 8. ECHOLOCAT*+IONS 10. SEWING (exch. *W* and *S*) 11. OEUVRE* 13. RESULT* 18. BOSS (2 defs.) 20. VIE+W+ER 22. BORNeo 26. SYM(P)TOM* 28. ME+NO+RAH 30. GENERA* 33. GNARL (odd letters) 34. L+ABEL 35. DO(N)OR 37. GIG+I 39. LO(C)O 40. C+O,O

Round-trip tour: Albuquerque, Evanston, Newark, Kenosha, Amarillo, Ossining, Gary, Yuma.

40

ACROSS: 1. SH+ERBE* 7. SHE(PR)D 13. COKIE 14. GER+KIN 16. TIN 18. TM(P)O* 19. HUm+KING 20. KEN 21. LI+IN+G 22. WO(OPE*)E 23. MAI(G)N 24. TI+MRS (*it* rev.) 25. EX(TEN)S* 26. CH(BB)+Y 27. O+S+E 28. TAP(I+O)A 29. GH'S+T 30. PESt 31. CHE(A)ER 32. AWFUL 33. UNLESS 34. LO+LARD

DOWN: 1. SOAP(BO)X)ES* 2. M(ALTHO')USE 3. P+E(KIN)GESE* 4. CA(RO)LLING (*or* rev.) 5. V+A+GU(EN)ESS 6. PAST(ICH*)ES 7. RE+LitIGIOUS 8. W(OR(K)B)ENCH 9. PYGMy+A+LION 10. TO+MA+HAWKS 11. P(ROF+IT)EER (*for* rev.) 12. UNDRE(SS)ED* 13. CAME+LOT 15. K(ITCH)EN 17. ST(ANLE*)Y

Letters omitted from Across clues spell "You've called all the shots"

41

ACROSS: 1. PIP+E 4. S(KIM+M)ILK 10. L(O,O)FAH* 12. D(EAR)IE 14. TOLL (2 defs.) 15. E+N(G)INE 16. S+TO A T 18. B(L)END 20. UMBRELLA* 22. INC (hid.) 23. ADORER* 24. H(ANGTO*)UGH 25. RO(O)M 27. C(APRI)C+IOUS 32. GE+ORG(I)AN (*e.g.* rev.) 33. TR...IX 34. RATS (hid.) 37. PERFUM*+E+S 39. A+MY 40. SI(X+TYNI*)NE 43. FIRE OPAL* 44. COM(PET)E 45. TROLL (2 defs.) 46. UNAIDED*

DOWN: 1. PL+AUDITS 2. 10[4]0 3. POLO (move *o* in *pool*) 4. SARTRE* 5. K+HYBER* 6. MEN(ELA)US (*ale* rev.) 7. IRIDIUM* 8. LIN+IN+G (*nil* rev.) 9. KEE(PI...)N+T+OUCH 11. F(L)AB 12. DEL+L (all rev.) 13. DAR(TAG)N+AN 17. TU(DO)Rkey 19. WARC+RAFT (*craw* rev.) 21. MOO+G 24. "HOUR" 26. MISS+A+L 27. C(A+PILL)ARIES 28. INEXCUSABLEf* 29. STUN (rev.) 30. NIENTE (hid.) 31. AX(SE)ED 35. A+MIR (*rim* rev.) 36. TYPO (hid.) 38. MISPRINTED* 41. T+ON 42. YMA (hid.)

Altered answers are made to fit the diagram by removing the name of an automobile.

42

NORTHWEST: 1. AE+RIAL (*lair* rev.) 2. A(R)TILY* 3. "BASEST" 4. B(R)ATTY 5. R(EAG*)AN 6. S(A+L)OON 7. S(A+T)IRE 8. TARP+ON

NORTHEAST: 9. AMUSED* 10. D+ODDER 11. ERO(TI)C (all rev.) 12. H(O)GTIE* 13. METE(O)R 14. M'TH(O,O)+D 15. SCOUTS* 16. VELCRO*

CENTER: 17. sCRIMPS 18. EG+ESTS* 19. INSIDE (hid.) 20. IN(S)URE 21. R(HUM)BA* 22. S(M)EARS 23. SO(I)RE+E 24. auSPICES

SOUTHWEST: 25. ANKARA (hid.) 26. C(R)ABBY 27. "ENNE+AD" 28. "EN+TREE" 29. HE(RA)LD 30. PE+ACHY 31. bRAMBLEs 32. Y+EAGER

SOUTHEAST: 33. A+BATES 34. BATBOYc* 35. CLEESE (*lee* for *a* in *case*) 36. F(E)ASTS 37. HONEST (hid.) 38. L+Y(N)XES (all rev.) 39. P+A+ROLE 40. V(ORTE*)+X

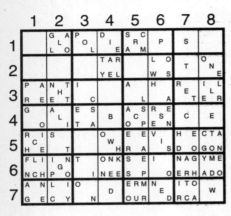

43

ROWS: 1. G(ALL)OP; O+L(D)IES; CRA(M)PS 2. TAR (2 defs.); YE+L+LO(W)ST+ONE 3. PARENT+HE(TIC)AL; "HARE"; TILLER (2 defs.) 4. GO+AL(I)ES; TA(BASs)CO; "PRESENCE" 5. RI(C)HES*; T(OWH*)EE; R+AVI(SHE)D; O(C...T+AG+O)N 6. FLIN(CHIN)G; POT+ION; K+NEES (*seen* rev.); E+SPION(A)GE*; RHYME (last letters); A+DO 7. ANGELIC*; Y+ON+DER (*red* rev.); MOURN (hid.); EDIT(O)R*; CAW (rev.)

COLUMNS: 1. PA(REGOR+I)C (all rev.); cHEF+LIN (*nil* rev.); CHANG+E 2. GALLeON; THE+TA; LISTING (2 defs.); PO(L+I)CY* 3. PO(LICE)ST+AT+IO+N 4. DI(ET)ARY; ELBOW (hid.); H+ON+K; NEE+D 5. S+CRAM; A+LASs; COP+E; ERAS+E; S+PERM; fOUR 6. P(LOW)SHAR*+E,S; EN(VI(S)I+ONE)D 7. ST...+RETCHED; O(NAG)'ER; H+IT; ORCA (hid.) 8. O'NEILL*; ERE+CT; A(GO)NY; ME(A)DOW*

44

ACROSS: 1. RETAR+DANCES (*rater* rev.) 8. ME+TROS (*sort* rev.) 9. ENVI*+SAGE 10. CORN+ERE+D 11. AS(LEE)P 12. PONTI*+AC 14. E+N(CL)AVE 17. LOC(A)T*+E 19. THIN+KING 21. V(E)T+ERANS (all rev.) 22. DE(P)AR+T 23. M+IN+DREADING

DOWN: 2. ESPRIT (move *E* in *sprite*) 3. RO(S)Y 4. "HEI DI" 5. C(A+VI)AR 6. SH(O)E 7. NE(T)W+EIGHT 8. MICROWAVE* 13. R(EM)AIN (*me* rev.) 15. ANIMAL (hid.) 16. POSER (2 defs.) 18. C+RAM 20. IOTA (hid.)

Lost and gained letters spell TRANSPLANTED.

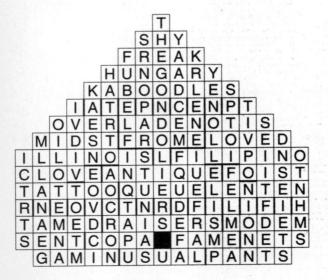

45

ACROSS: 4. COP+A 10. PANTS (2 defs.) 17. F(I)LIP+IN+O 34. ILLIN'+O+I 36. FROM+E 42. "FOIST" 43. MODE+M 47. FR(E)A*+K 48. "RAISERS" 51 FAME (hid.) 60. KABOODLES* 71. OTIS* 72. NETS (rev.) 88. US+U+AL 105. HUNG(A)RY 109. TA(ME)D 114. OVER (hid.) 118. L+A+DEN 121 TAT+TOO 126. MID+ST (*dim* rev.) 128. LENTEN (hid.) 139. "QUEUE" 144 CLOVE (2 defs.) 146. LOVED (hid. rev.) 162. SENTence 166. mAN+TIQUE 168. GAMINg 171. SHYlock

DOWN: 2. N+IN ON 13. THE GONDOLIERS 17. QUA(FF+E)D 19. TOP(I)S 34. ST+RI+CT 42. FE+MALE 46. DES(TIN)ES* 47. BUFF+L+E 59 A(CAD)E+MY 60. S+NAKEd 61. FA+I+LURE 77. TEST(IF+I)ED 81. MOTE+ 86. SIMPLE (hid.) 89. S(US)TAIN 105. TH(R+O)AT 108. PI(QUA)NT 112 PIV+OT (all rev.) 113. VI(V)I+D 114. EMOT+I+ON+A+L (all rev.) 126 MA(GELLA*)N 137. M(ON)'THS 166. C+OR+ON+A 170. VOI(CE)D 171 SP(ORR)AN 176. LONELY (hid. rev.) 177. "KERNEL"

Quotation: In a contemplative fashion, / And a tranquil frame of mind, / Free from every kind of passion, / Some solution let us find. / Let us grasp the situation, Solve the complicated plot / Quiet, calm deliberation / Disentangles every knot
— W. S. Gilbert, *The Gondoliers*